The Critical Idiom
General Editor: JOHN D. JUMP

24 The Grotesque

In the same series

The Grotesque/*Philip Thomson*

Methuen & Co Ltd

PN
56
G7
T5

First published 1972
by Methuen & Co Ltd
11 New Fetter Lane, London EC4
© *1972 Philip Thomson*
Printed in Great Britain
by Cox & Wyman Ltd, Fakenham, Norfolk

SBN 416 98170 3 Hardback
SBN 416 08180 0 Paperback

Distributed in the U.S.A.
by Barnes & Noble Inc.

Contents

General Editor's Preface

This volume is one of a series of short studies, each dealing with a single key item, or a group of two or three key items, in our critical vocabulary. The purpose of the series differs from that served by the standard glossaries of literary terms. Many terms are adequately defined for the needs of students by the brief entries in these glossaries, and such terms will not be the subjects of studies in the present series. But there are other terms which cannot be made familiar by means of compact definitions. Students need to grow accustomed to them through simple and straightforward but reasonably full discussions of them. The purpose of this series is to provide such discussions.

Some of the terms in question refer to literary movements (e.g., 'Romanticism', 'Aestheticism', etc.), others to literary kinds (e.g., 'Comedy', 'Epic', etc.), and still others to stylistic features (e.g., 'Irony', 'The Conceit', etc.). Because of this diversity of subject-matter, no attempt has been made to impose a uniform pattern upon the studies. But all authors have tried to provide as full illustrative quotation as possible, to make reference whenever appropriate to more than one literature, and to compose their studies in such a way as to guide readers towards the short bibliographies in which they have made suggestions for further reading.

John D. Jump

University of Manchester

Acknowledgements

I should like to thank my colleagues in the Faculty of Arts at Monash University, Melbourne, especially Mr D. C. Muecke, for their help and criticism while I was writing this study, and my editor Professor J. D. Jump for his valuable suggestions.

I

Introduction

In Samuel Beckett's novel *Watt* there is a description of a remarkable family called Lynch, which reads in part as follows:

> There was Tom Lynch, widower, aged eighty-five years, confined to his bed with constant undiagnosed pains in the caecum, and his three surviving boys Joe, aged sixty-five years, a rheumatic cripple, and Jim, aged sixty-four years, a hunchbacked inebriate, and Bill, widower, aged sixty-three years, greatly hampered in his movements by the loss of both legs as the result of a slip, followed by a fall, and his only surviving daughter May Sharpe, widow, aged sixty-two years, in full possession of all her faculties with the exception of that of vision. Then there was Joe's wife *née* Doyly-Byrne, aged sixty-five years, a sufferer from Parkinson's palsy but otherwise very fit and well, and Jim's wife Kate *née* Sharpe aged sixty-four years, covered all over with running sores of an unidentified nature but otherwise fit and well. Then there was Joe's boy Tom aged forty-one years, unfortunately subject alternately to fits of exaltation, which rendered him incapable of the least exertion, and of depression, during which he could stir neither hand nor foot, and Bill's boy Sam, aged forty years, paralysed by a merciful providence from no higher than the knees down and from no lower than the waist up, and May's spinster daughter Ann, aged thirty-nine years, greatly reduced in health and spirits by a painful congenital disorder of an unmentionable kind, and Jim's lad Jack aged thirty-eight years, who was weak in the head, and the boon twins Art and Con aged thirty-seven years, who measured in height when in their stockinged feet three feet and four inches and who weighed in weight when stripped to the buff seventy-one pounds all bone and sinew and between whom the resemblance was so marked in every way that even those (and they were many) who knew and loved them most would call Art Con when they meant Art, and Con

Art when they meant Con, as least as often as, if not more often than, they called Art Art when they meant Art, and Con Con when they meant Con. And then there was young Tom's wife Mag *née* Sharpe aged forty-one years, greatly handicapped in her house and outdoor activity by subepileptic seizures of monthly incidence, during which she rolled foaming on the floor or on the yard, or on the vegetable patch, or on the river's brim, and seldom failed to damage herself in one way or another, so that she was obliged to go to bed, and remain there, every month, until she was better, and Sam's wife Liz *née* Sharpe, aged thirty-eight years, fortunate in being more dead than alive as a result of having in the course of twenty years given Sam nineteen children, of whom four survived, and again expecting, and poor Jack who it will be remembered was weak in the head his wife Lil *née* Sharpe aged thirty-eight years, who was weak in the chest.

(Grove Press edition, New York, 1959, pp. 101–2)

We may well ask ourselves what our response to this passage is, or ought to be. The question is likely to arise because chances are that the reader's reaction will be somewhat confused, or at least divided. He will presumably respond to the tragic, disgusting or deformed nature of the unfortunate Lynches with a certain amount of horror, pity – perhaps even nausea. On the other hand the undoubtedly comic aspect of the description will rather induce him to respond with amusement or mirth. Indeed, it may be difficult to resolve this conflict in response. Re-reading may serve only to reinforce what is essentially a clash between incompatible reactions – laughter on the one hand and horror or disgust on the other. In seeking to explain this peculiar mixture in our response, we might point to a similar clash in the text itself, between – on the most obvious level – the gruesome or horrifying content and the comic manner in which it is presented. And in searching for words to convey this clash we should probably come up – along with a number of other more or less accurate descriptions – with the word 'grotesque', if only on the vague basis by which the same word in phrases such as 'a grotesque scene' conveys the notion of simultaneously laughable and horrifying or disgusting. What will be generally agreed upon, in other words, is that 'grotesque' will cover, perhaps among other things, the co-presence of the laughable and something which is incompatible with the laughable.

A further point needs to be made about our reaction to Beckett's text. After the initial response to this passage, which as I have suggested will be essentially divided, the reader may well do one of two things as a further reaction. He may decide that the passage is more funny than horrifying, he may 'laugh it off' or treat it as a joke; alternatively, he may be indignant and regard it as an outrage to his moral sensibilities that such things should be presented in a humorous light. Both these secondary responses, if I may term them such, are highly interesting psychologically, and we shall have occasion to return to them. Suffice to say for the present that they both involve rationalization and defence-mechanisms, suggesting that the grotesque (assuming that this is in fact what we are confronted with) is hard to take, and that we tend to try to escape the discomfort it causes.

The reader who remains caught in his initial reaction or who does not allow secondary considerations to colour his response, may decide that nothing can be gained by regarding the above passage in isolation and that, if it were put in context, the tone of the whole thing and therefore one's response would be made clear and straightforward. Any reader moderately familiar with *Watt*, or with the work of Beckett in general, will of course know that this is not the case. On the contrary, the more 'context' one adds to a given passage the more uncertain one becomes.

One other potential misconception needs to be met at this stage. It may be felt, both in relation to the above passage and generally, that there is no point to the grotesque, that it is a gratuitous mixing together of incompatible elements for its own sake, or for no other purpose than to bewilder the reader. But while this may be the case with some instances of the grotesque, it is dangerous to generalize. Some of the most notable uses of the grotesque occur in the work of Swift, and here it is quite clear that the grotesque is being calculatingly employed in the service of something which has a definite purpose – satire, in the main. This is the case, for example, with *A Modest Proposal*, a piece which begins in seemingly innocent fashion with the speaker deploring the large numbers of neglected and unemployable waifs in Ireland, and, in the manner of a mathematician or an economist, presenting certain calculations intended to illuminate this sorry state of affairs. The initiated or discerning reader will fairly quickly see that Swift is adopting the tone and manner of the economist for a purpose: he is able to make good capital out of the contrast between this dry, pedantic manner and the horrifying conditions he describes. It is very doubtful, however, whether any reader is prepared for the proposal itself, which is presented with shocking suddenness:

> I shall now therefore humbly propose my own Thoughts, which I hope will not be liable to the least Objection. I have been assured by a very knowing American of my acquaintance in London, that a young healthy Child well Nursed is at a Year Old a most delicious nourishing and wholesome Food, whether Stewed, Roasted, Baked, or Boiled; and I make no doubt that it will equally serve in a Fricasie, or a Ragoust.
>
> I do therefore humbly offer it to publick consideration, that of the Hundred and twenty thousand Children, already computed, twenty thousand may be reserved for Breed, whereof only one fourth part to be Males; which is more than we allow to Sheep, black Cattle, or Swine, and my Reason is, that these Children are seldom the Fruits of Marriage, a Circumstance not much regarded by our Savages, therefore, one Male will be sufficient to serve four Females. That the remaining Hundred thousand may at a year Old be offered in Sale to the Persons of Quality and Fortune, through the Kingdom, always advising the Mother to let them Suck plentifully in the last Month, so

as to render them Plump, and Fat for a good Table. A Child will make two Dishes at an Entertainment for Friends, and when the Family dines alone, the fore and hind Quarter will make a reasonable Dish, and seasoned with a little Pepper or Salt will be very good Boiled on the fourth Day, especially in Winter.

Here again one's response is likely to be confused. Horror will certainly be present in it, but surely also delight in the savage wit of Swift and a mirthful reaction to the utter incongruity between the appalling substance of the proposal and the reasonable, sober manner in which it is put. A full response to this text, I suggest, will not allow the mirth to be blotted out by the horror, or vice versa. Both will remain, in a state of tension. One might speculate, indeed, whether the comic element does not in effect make the whole thing even more shocking, even more difficult to stomach. An interesting point about the passage is that one's horror is not really diminished by the knowledge that Swift is not serious; that is, the intellectual awareness of what Swift is up to is unable to prevent the emotional impact of the proposal. This suggests that the effect of the grotesque is at least as strongly emotional as it is intellectual. It is also worth noting that the incongruity mentioned above as comic is also the source of additional horror; that is, the grisly nature of the proposal is bad enough, but the mild and reasonable tone in which it is put makes it worse. This is important: it indicates that the extreme incongruity associated with the grotesque is itself ambivalent in that it is both comic and monstrous.

It may be objected that the notion of the grotesque so far advanced takes no account of an aspect which is felt by some people to be essential: the aspect, namely, of eeriness, of the spine-chillingly uncanny. While I am not at all sure that this is a necessary element in the grotesque, it may be expedient to consider now a third passage, from the beginning of Franz Kafka's story *The Metamorphosis*:

As Gregor Samsa awoke one morning from uneasy dreams he found himself transformed in his bed into a gigantic insect. He was lying on his hard, as it were, armour-plated, back and when he lifted his head a little he could see his dome-like brown belly divided into stiff arched segments on top of which the bed-quilt could hardly keep in position and was about to slide off completely. His numerous legs, which were pitifully thin compared to the rest of his bulk, waved helplessly before his eyes.

What has happened to me? he thought. It was no dream. His room, a regular human bedroom, only rather too small, lay quiet between the four familiar walls. Above the table on which a collection of cloth samples was unpacked and spread out – Samsa was a commercial traveller – hung the picture which he had recently cut out of an illustrated magazine and put into a pretty gilt frame. It showed a lady, with a fur cap on and a fur stole, sitting upright and holding out to the spectator a huge fur muff into which the whole of her forearm had vanished.

Gregor's eyes turned next to the window, and the overcast sky – one could hear raindrops beating on the window gutter – made him quite melancholy. What about sleeping a little longer and forgetting all this nonsense, he thought, but it could not be done, for he was accustomed to sleep on his right side and in his present condition he could not turn himself over. However violently he forced himself towards his right side he always rolled on to his back again. He tried it at least a hundred times, shutting his eyes to keep from seeing his struggling legs, and only desisted when he began to feel in his side a faint dull ache he had never experienced before.

O God, he thought, what an exhausting job I've picked on! Travelling about day in, day out. It's much more irritating work than doing the actual business in the warehouse, and on top of that there's the trouble of constant travelling, of worrying about train connections, the bed and irregular meals, casual acquaintances that are always new and never become intimate friends. The devil take it all! He felt a slight itching up on his belly; slowly pushed himself on his back nearer to the top of the bed so that he could lift his head more easily; identified the itching place which was surrounded by many small white spots the nature of which he could not understand, and made to

touch it with a leg, but drew the leg back immediately, for the contact
made a cold shiver run through him.

(trans. by W. and E. Muir, Penguin, Harmondsworth, 1963)

Whether or not this is felt to be eerie, I suggest that once again the
crucial factor in one's reaction to it is the confusion between a
sense of the comic and something – revulsion, horror, fear – which
is incompatible with the comic. And here also, this confusion
corresponds to a thorough-going mixture of incompatibles in the
text. Gregor is a human being, but at the same time a monstrous
insect; he thinks like a man, but has the human-sized body of a
repulsive type of vermin (the English 'insect' does not render the
nastiness of *Ungeziefer* in the original German). Gregor's matter-
of-fact attitude and trivial thoughts stand in ludicrous – but some-
how also terrifying – contrast to his monstrous predicament.
There is a constant interplay, carried on for several more pages,
between Gregor's banal worries about everyday matters and
references to his terrible physical situation. Not least, Kafka's way
of turning away from Gregor himself, after the initial startling
paragraph, to indulge in a seemingly pointless description of the
uninteresting room, and the cool, quiet, factual tone of the narra-
tive in general, are extremely inappropriate.

As for 'eerie', we may well apply the word to such a passage, to
cover a mixture of epithets like 'weird', 'frightening', 'mysterious'
and so on. But I suggest that unless we take 'eerie' to contain also
some suggestion of the comic – and this would be most unusual –
it is not the most appropriate word, as it covers only one aspect of
the passage. This must be the objection, indeed, to those views of
the grotesque as something essentially uncanny and unnatural.
There is a further danger here also, that one could be misled into
associating the grotesque too closely with the fantastic. The
relationship between the two is complicated, and we shall be
obliged to dwell on it at a later stage, but it is interesting to note in
the above passage that, however unnatural and impossible the

metamorphosis which Kafka describes, it is narrated in an entirely realistic, indeed matter-of-fact fashion, as if it were a quite ordinary event. Kafka is at pains to prevent our taking his story on the level of a fairy-tale, horror-story, tale of the supernatural or fantastic, and he explicitly says 'It was no dream'. The story is not situated in the realm of the fantastic, and the reader does not respond to it in this way: on the contrary. We can take it, then, as likely that, far from possessing a necessary affinity with the fantastic, the grotesque derives at least some of its effect from being presented within a realistic framework, in a realistic way.

My insistence on the comic aspect of the beginning of *The Metamorphosis* should not be taken as an attempt to deny in any way the horror of Kafka's story. On the contrary, as mentioned earlier, the intrusion of the comic element, totally out of place and inappropriate, serves to increase the reader's sense of the frightful nature of these scenes. We feel that this mixture of horror and comedy is 'impossible', we cannot be reconciled to it, we may even feel it is indecent and indicative of a warped mind – but we are unable to shake off the profoundly disturbing effect which it has on us.

One further factor common to the three examples so far offered is worth noting, namely the *physical* nature of the events and descriptions presented – physical in each case in an immediate and vivid way. Beckett's diseased and deformed Lynch family, the very concrete details of Swift's proposal for serving up children at dinner, and Gregor's metamorphosis all involve the human body in a quite direct way, and we are probably safe in surmising that a good deal of the effect of these passages has to do with the palpable detail in which they are presented. Certain problems are raised by this, the most important being the possibility that our laughter at some kinds of the grotesque and the opposite response – disgust, horror, etc. – mixed with it, are both reactions to the physically cruel, abnormal or obscene; the possibility, in other words, that alongside our civilized response something deep within us, some area of our unconscious, some hidden but very much alive sadistic impulse makes us react to such things with unholy glee and barbaric delight. Just how far one can legitimately pursue this aspect of the grotesque is doubtful, but we may note that, at the very least, the grotesque has a strong affinity with the *physically abnormal*.

2
The Term and Concept 'Grotesque': A Historical Summary

The three passages offered above and the discussion of them reflect, necessarily, a contemporary understanding of the grotesque. I have tried to keep to examples of and notions about the grotesque on which there is general agreement among modern writers on the subject, although this is not easy. But a discussion of the grotesque cannot afford to ignore the historical development of the word 'grotesque' and its usage, and the various previous concepts of what is meant by the term, particularly as some of these older notions are still accepted (rightly or wrongly). The application of the term in the eighteenth century is likely to be markedly different from its use in the nineteenth, and both can be expected to be different from our present usage. These past uses of the word, however, can be extremely helpful in reaching our own understanding of the grotesque, even if we decline to take them over *in toto*. It is even possible to gain valuable insights into our subject from earlier conceptions which we completely reject. Accordingly, it will prove helpful to suspend at this point our consideration of the three examples presented in order to trace briefly the development of the word and concept 'grotesque'.

Literary terms, particularly those denoting categories and modes of writing, are constantly in need of repair and renewal. They become worn, their application becomes loose or distorted by a variety of factors ranging from over-subjectivity on the part of the individuals using them to the particular tastes of a given historical era. The grotesque has suffered even more than most from this inevitable variation, perhaps because of its radical and extreme nature; indeed, only recently has there been agreement on whether 'the grotesque' is a valid and meaningful term at all. Despite some notable, but isolated, attempts in the nineteenth century to define the nature of the grotesque, it was not until the appearance in 1957 of the book by the late German critic Wolfgang Kayser, *The Grotesque in Art and Literature*, that the grotesque became the object of considerable aesthetic analysis and critical evaluation. Where previous ages had seen in it merely the principle of disharmony run wild, or relegated it to the cruder species of the comic, the present tendency – one which must be welcomed as a considerable step forward – is to view the grotesque as a fundamentally ambivalent thing, as a violent clash of opposites, and hence, in some of its forms at least, as an appropriate expression of the problematical nature of existence. It is no accident that the grotesque mode in art and literature tends to be prevalent in societies and eras marked by strife, radical change or disorientation. Although one runs the risk of succumbing to clichés when one regards the past forty or fifty years as just such an era convulsed by momentous social and intellectual changes, it can nevertheless be fairly said that this is an important contributing factor in the present artistic situation, where the grotesque is very much in evidence. Even a quick random sampling of what is being currently produced – with such names as Harold Pinter and Joe Orton in England, J. P. Donleavy and John Barth in the U.S.A., Samuel Beckett and Eugene Ionesco in France, Günter Grass in Germany and Friedrich Dürrenmatt in Switzerland – will attest to the extent to which the grotesque has become a favoured mode in world literature. This is not to speak of the other arts, where a similar situation prevails.

The grotesque is not of course a phenomenon solely of the twentieth century, nor even of modern civilization. It existed as an artistic mode in the West at least as far back as the early Christian period of Roman culture, where there evolved a style of combining human, animal and vegetable elements, intricately interwoven, in the one painting. The German art historian Ludwig Curtius quotes the comments of the Roman writer Marcus Vitruvius Pollio, writing during the reign of Augustus, on this new style:

... For our contemporary artists decorate the walls with monstrous forms rather than reproducing clear images of the familiar world. Instead of columns they paint fluted stems with oddly shaped leaves and volutes, and instead of pediments arabesques; the same with candelabra and painted edifices, on the pediments of which grow dainty flowers unrolling out of robes and topped, without rhyme or reason, by little figures. The little stems, finally, support half-figures crowned by human or animal heads. Such things, however, never existed, do not now exist, and shall never come into being.

... For how can the stem of a flower support a roof, or a candelabrum bear pedimental sculpture? How can a tender shoot carry a human figure, and how can bastard forms composed of flowers and human bodies grow out of roots and tendrils?

(Quoted by Kayser, p. 20)

Two things are worth noting about this description. First, the main characteristic of this style is the confusion of heterogeneous elements, the interweaving of plant, animal, human and architectural forms. It is also strongly implied that Vitruvius finds this confusion both monstrous and ludicrous. Second, the attitude of the worthy Vitruvius is one of indignant rejection. He, the classical-minded critic, is outraged by the wilful disregard of the principle of mimesis or realistic reproduction of the familiar world, and by the transgression against the laws of nature and proportion. It is an attitude towards the grotesque which has been common ever since, particularly in ages where classical notions of art and literature prevail.

Murals of the kind described by Vitruvius first came to light around 1500 in the course of excavations in Rome. From *grotte* (Ital. 'caves', thus by extension 'excavations') came the adjective *grottesco* and the noun *la grottesca*, denoting the kind of painting discussed above. The word *crotesque* occurs in French as early as 1532, and is used in English as well before being replaced around 1640 by *grotesque*. Early usages of the word in English are restricted to the antique paintings and to the imitations of this style which became popular in the sixteenth century, particularly in Italy (cf. the grotesques of Raphael). The extension of the word 'grotesque' to literature and to non-artistic things took place in France as early as the sixteenth-century (Rabelais uses it with reference to parts of the body), but in England and Germany only in the eighteenth century. With this extension 'grotesque' took on a broader meaning. In particular its association with caricature – a topic much discussed by eighteenth-century aestheticians – led to what Kayser calls a loss of substance in the word, meaning the suppression of the horrifying or eerie qualities of the grotesque and a corresponding over-emphasis on the ridiculous and bizarre. Arthur Clayborough, in his book *The Grotesque in English Literature* (1965), also notes this development:

> The word grotesque thus comes to be applied in a more general fashion during the Age of Reason – and of Neo-Classicism – when the characteristics of the grotesque style of art – extravagance, fantasy, individual taste, and the rejection of 'the natural conditions of organization' – are the object of ridicule and disapproval. The more general sense ... which it has developed by the early eighteenth century is therefore that of 'ridiculous, distorted, unnatural' (adj.); 'an absurdity, a distortion of nature' (noun).
>
> (p. 6)

These pejorative connotations of the grotesque persisted, alongside the original technical meaning of a particular type of painting, into the nineteenth century and indeed to a large extent into the twentieth. Even those writers well-disposed towards the grotesque tended to treat it as a vulgar species of the comic, closely allied to the burlesque and to caricature. In Germany, both Justus Moser in

Harlekin oder die Verteidigung des Grotesk-Komischen (Harlequin or The Defence of the Grotesquely Comic, 1761) and F. Th. Vischer in his *Aesthetics* of 1857 deprive the grotesque in this way of its more serious qualities. The same may be said of John Addington Symonds (*Caricature, the Fantastic, the Grotesque*, 1890) and Thomas Wright (*A History of Caricature and Grotesque in Literature and Art*, 1865), although the latter does not entirely deny the presence of the horrifying or disgusting in the grotesque. Another German, Heinrich Schneegans, whose *Geschichte der grotesken Satire* (History of Grotesque Satire, 1894) concentrates largely on Rabelais, likewise treats the grotesque in terms of ludicrous exaggeration.

Kayser and others have rightly objected to this view of the grotesque as exaggerated buffoonery or the ludicrously fantastic on the grounds that it fails to take account of the many instances of a *co-presence* of the ludicrous with the monstrous, the disgusting or the horrifying. Whether these instances are to be found in the paintings of Bosch and Brueghel or in Goya's *Disasters of War*, or in the writings of Swift, Blake, E. T. A. Hoffmann and even the more savage passages of the usually jolly Rabelais, they cannot be explained, or even usefully apprehended, by reference merely to outrageous exaggeration.

It is perhaps easier for us, living in the second half of the twentieth century, to make this criticism and insist on a component of horror or something similar in the grotesque. It may be said that our notion of the grotesque is conditioned by the many examples from modern and contemporary literature of the comic inexplicably combined with the monstrous, of the interweaving of totally disparate elements, producing a strange and often unpleasant and unsettling conflict of emotions. Yet there are several writers of the eighteenth and nineteenth centuries who emphasize the serious and powerfully unsettling nature of the grotesque. These writers include such unlike natures as John Ruskin and Victor Hugo,

Friedrich Schlegel and Walter Bagehot, but they all have in common the tendency to see in the grotesque something more than outlandish exaggeration or wild burlesque. Even the classical-minded Victorian Bagehot, who makes no bones, in his essay 'Wordsworth, Tennyson, and Browning; or, Pure, Ornate, and Grotesque Art in English Poetry' (1864), about preferring pure to ornate and both to grotesque art, is ready to admit the legitimacy of the grotesque as a kind of negative example, the other side of the coin to the beautiful and sublime. For Ruskin, on the other hand, some types of grotesque, in the hands of noble men with true spiritual awareness (Dante, for example), are great, and may take their place with all but the very highest examples of art. In the chapter entitled 'Grotesque Renaissance' in *The Stones of Venice* (1851–3) Ruskin distinguishes between 'noble' or 'true' grotesque and 'ignoble' or 'false' grotesque, the former being associated with the realization of man's tragic and imperfect nature, the latter with wilful frivolity. Although we would perhaps reject the moralistic overtones of Ruskin's analysis, his work is noteworthy for the stress he places on the playful or sportive element in the grotesque. All grotesque art is for him partly a product of a specially strong urge to play, invent, manipulate – to experiment, we might say.

We may note two further points of interest in Ruskin's essay. He insists on the combination of the ludicrous and the terrible in the grotesque, and he associates the latter element with horror, anger or awe at the human condition. Just how the two elements – the ludicrous and the terrible – come to be combined is not made very clear, but it is interesting to observe that the idea of the terrible, specifically the metaphysically terrible, crops up again in Kayser's notion of the grotesque.

Ruskin was by no means the first to emphasize the play element in the grotesque. The German Romantic theorist Friedrich Schlegel, in his *Gespräch über die Poesie* (Conversation on Poetry, 1800), had spoken of the fecund imagination which the grotesque manifests, and from his theoretical writings in general it is clear that playfulness is an important ingredient in all those things the Romantics praised: as well as the grotesque and the 'arabesque' (the distinction between these is never made clear), the ironic, the paradoxical and the fantastic. Indeed for Schlegel all these modes – if we may call them such – overlap. Kayser, referring to the earlier Schlegel fragments in the first volume of the *Athenäum*, summarizes:

> According to fragments 75, 305 and 389, grotesqueness is constituted by a clashing contrast between form and content, the unstable mixture of heterogeneous elements, the explosive force of the paradoxical, which is both ridiculous and terrifying.
>
> (p. 53)

Friedrich Schlegel makes approving reference to the German novelist Jean Paul (Friedrich Richter) as a grotesque writer. Interestingly Jean Paul, in his own theoretical work *Vorschule der Ästhetik* (Primer of Aesthetics, 1804), has a section dealing with what he calls '*die vernichtende Idee des Humors*' (the annihilating idea of humour), by which he means that type of humour which is painful, awesome, which knows of evil and the abyss. Jean Paul thus adds a further factor to Schlegel's analysis of the grotesque, emphasizing the dark and terrible nature of some kinds of humour. Both his novels and his theoretical writings place Jean Paul firmly in the tradition of satanic and black humour – a tradition which continues to produce some of the best examples of the grotesque.

The most sustained Romantic discourse on the grotesque comes not from Germany but from France. Victor Hugo's preface to his drama *Cromwell* (1827), intended as a programme for a new (i.e. Romantic) kind of literature, is devoted largely to a discussion of the grotesque as the characteristic mode of modern – as against pre-Romantic – art. Much of what Hugo has to say has already been touched on above in connection with other writers on the grotesque, but we should note his insistence that the grotesque, transmitted through the medium of comic drama, is to be the hall-mark of literature henceforth. Hugo thus removes the grotesque from the fringes of artistic creation to a position of centrality, stressing the infinite variety in the comic, the horrible and the ugly – the latter is especially important to him – compared to the narrow confines of the beautiful and sublime. It is also worth noting that Hugo associates the grotesque not with the fantastic but with the realistic, making it clear that the grotesque is not just an artistic mode or category but exists in nature and in the world around us.

This last point – an extremely important one, for it shifts the grotesque into the realm of realistic as against fantastic art – is also made by G. K. Chesterton in his book *Robert Browning* (1903). Chesterton asserts, as Clayborough puts it, 'that the grotesque may be employed as a means of presenting the world in a new light without falsifying it', i.e. that it may be a function of the grotesque to make us see the (real) world anew, from a fresh perspective which, though it be a strange and disturbing one, is nevertheless valid and realistic. This is a notion which gains importance in the twentieth century and one which will bear examination when we come to the concept of alienation.

Chesterton looks at the grotesque in three ways: as a reflection of the real world, as an artistic mode and as the product of a certain kind of temperament. The latter consideration involves of course psychological analysis and speculation, an approach which brings obvious dangers with it as one must rely on getting at the gro-tesque through the mental make-up and artistic temperament of the author. However, several attempts of this kind have been made, the most notable being Clayborough's use of Jungian psychology to analyse the grotesque elements in Swift, Coleridge and Dickens. Clayborough operates with two pairs of opposites: progressive and regressive, and positive and negative. Progressive art is associated with a predominance of the conscious mind in the creative process, regressive art with a predominance of the un-conscious. Positive art is art where no inner conflict is felt, where the presentation of truth or reality proceeds harmoniously, nega-tive art the opposite. For Clayborough, the two kinds of art which have the most affinity with the grotesque are the regressive–negative and the progressive–negative, the former being linked with subjective, non-directed grotesquery (surrealism is men-tioned in this connection), the latter with grotesquery used as a tool of satire or as a shock tactic.

Though it would be unkind to say that Clayborough's termino-logy confuses rather than illuminates, his treatment of the gro-tesque really amounts to no more than a re-statement, in different terms, of the fairly well-established fact that the grotesque is essentially disharmonious, depending on conflict of some sort, and that it may be either the expression of a profound sense of dis-location and alienation or employed as an aggressive device in the service of satire and the like.

The most thorough attempt to define the nature of the gro-tesque is Wolfgang Kayser's book, which comes to the following conclusions:

The grotesque is the expression of the estranged or alienated world, i.e. the familiar world is seen from a perspective which suddenly renders it strange (and, presumably, this strangeness may be either comic or terrifying, or both).

The grotesque is a game with the absurd, in the sense that the grotesque artist plays, half laughingly, half horrified, with the deep absurdities of existence.

The grotesque is an attempt to control and exorcise ('*zu bannen und zu beschwören*') the demonic elements in the world.

Kayser thus offers not so much a definition of the grotesque as a list of overlapping properties. We may object also to the some-what melodramatic over-emphasis on the 'demonic', which totally removes the fearsome aspect of the grotesque to the realm of the irrational – almost of the supernatural. But the real value of his book is greater than his conclusions may indicate. In particular, he was the first to insist that the grotesque can be seen, must be seen if it is to be meaningful as an aesthetic category, as 'a comprehensive structural principle'. The implication of this, which Kayser himself does not always follow, is that there must be a certain pattern peculiar to the grotesque, a certain fundamental structure which is perceivable in the grotesque work of art and its effect, as there is in parody, say, or – to take a more complicated example – in irony.

3
Towards a Definition

Before an attempt is made to further define this pattern, however, it may be helpful to summarize the main points to emerge from the preceding survey. It is obvious that 'grotesque' does not have a constant meaning, but we may distinguish certain recurring notions about it. In so doing, we shall try to move closer to an adequate modern definition of the grotesque.

DISHARMONY

The most consistently distinguished characteristic of the grotesque has been the fundamental element of disharmony, whether this is referred to as conflict, clash, mixture of the heterogeneous, or conflation of disparates. It is important that this disharmony has been seen, not merely in the work of art as such, but also in the reaction it produces and (speculatively) in the creative temperament and psychological make-up of the artist.

THE COMIC AND THE TERRIFYING

Writers on the grotesque have always tended to associate the grotesque with either the comic or the terrifying. Those who see it as a sub-form of the comic class the grotesque, broadly, with the burlesque and the vulgarly funny. Those who emphasize the terrifying quality of the grotesque often shift it towards the realm of the uncanny, the mysterious, even the supernatural. There are naturally a good many positions between these two poles, but, apart from a few exceptions in earlier periods, the tendency to view the grotesque as essentially a mixture in some way or other of *both* the comic and the terrifying (or the disgusting, repulsive, etc.) in a problematical (i.e. not readily resolvable) way is a comparatively recent one. We should emphasize the last part of this description of the grotesque: the special impact of the grotesque will be lacking if the conflict is resolved, if the text concerned proves to be just funny after all, or if it turns out that the reader has been quite mistaken in his initial perception of comedy in what is in fact stark horror. The *unresolved* nature of the grotesque conflict is important, and helps to mark off the grotesque from other modes or categories of literary discourse. For the conflict of incompatibles, fundamental though it be, is not exclusively a criterion of the grotesque. Irony and paradox depend on this sort of conflict or confrontation, and all theories of the comic are based on some notion of incongruity, conflict, juxtaposition of opposites, etc. We shall later investigate more closely the distinctions between the grotesque and these other modes, but we may confidently take it that the lack of resolution of the conflict is a distinguishing feature of the grotesque.

Of course, the mixture of the comic and the terrifying may be disproportionate, so that we have a case of a basically comic text with a very slight element of the frightening, or vice versa. In such cases the use of the term 'grotesque' may be debatable. In Dylan Thomas's *Under Milk Wood* there is a description of the would-be poisoner Mr Pugh planning to rid himself of his nagging wife:

> Alone in the hissing laboratory of his wishes, Mr Pugh minces among bad vats and jeroboams, tiptoes through spinneys of murdering herbs, agony dancing in his crucibles, and mixes especially for Mrs Pugh a venomous porridge unknown to toxicologists which will scald and viper through her until her ears fall off like figs, her toes grow big and black as balloons, and steam comes screaming out of her navel.
>
> (J. M. Dent, paperback edition, London, 1962, p. 63)

Do we feel here that the element of terror exists, or is present strongly enough to seriously conflict with the overall comic mood? Conversely, is there a comic element in the following scene from Joseph Heller's *Catch - 22* where the pilot McWatt is 'buzzing' a bathing beach?

> He studied every floating object fearfully for some gruesome sign of Clevinger and Orr, prepared for any morbid shock but the shock McWatt gave him one day with the plane that came blasting suddenly into sight out of the distant stillness and hurtled mercilessly along the shore line with a great growling, clattering roar over the bobbing raft on which blond, pale Kid Sampson, his naked sides scrawny even from so far away, leaped clownishly up to touch it at the exact moment some arbitrary gust of wind or minor miscalculation of McWatt's senses dropped the speeding plane down just low enough for a propeller to slice him half away.
>
> Even people who were not there remembered vividly exactly what happened next. There was the briefest, softest tsst! filtering audibly through the shattering, overwhelming howl of the plane's engines, and then there were just Kid Sampson's two pale, skinny legs, still joined by strings somehow at the bloody truncated hips, standing stock-still on the raft for what seemed a full minute or two before they toppled over backward into the water finally with a faint, echoing splash and turned completely upside down so that only the grotesque toes and the plaster-white soles of Kid Sampson's feet remained in view.
>
> (Corgi paperback edition, New York, 1964, p. 359)

We may even focus the question more narrowly and put it slightly differently: does Heller's reference to 'the grotesque toes' imply only a terrifying unnaturalness, or an element of comedy as well – a comedy so ghastly that we scarcely dare to give it the name?

EXTRAVAGANCE AND EXAGGERATION

It has always been generally agreed that the grotesque is extravagant, that it has a marked element of exaggeration, of extreme-ness, about it. This quality has often led to the association of the grotesque with the fantastic and fanciful. But we should be careful here: what Vitruvius and sundry later (mostly disapproving) classical-minded writers call the fantastic does not necessarily accord with our modern notion of it. As we noted previously, if 'fantastic' means simply a pronounced divergence from the normal and natural then the grotesque is undoubtedly fantastic. But if, as we surely must, we insist that the criterion be whether the material is presented in a fantastic, or realistic way, then we are more likely to conclude that, far from possessing an affinity with the fantastic, it is precisely the conviction that the grotesque world, however strange, is yet our world, real and immediate, which makes the grotesque so powerful. Even *The Metamorphosis*, in which the central event is 'impossible', will, as we have seen, bear this out.

Conversely, if a literary text 'takes place' in a fantasy-world created by the author, with no pretensions to a connection with reality, the grotesque is almost out of the question. For within a closed fantasy-world, anything is possible. The reader, once he is aware that he is confronted with such a closed world, accepts the strangest things without turning a hair, for he is not being asked to understand them as real. Gerhard Mensching, in a dissertation entitled *Das Groteske im modernen Drama* (The Grotesque in Modern Drama, 1961), rightly emphasizes this distinction:

> No matter how inventive the author of the fantastic is, he will mostly keep to the perspective of the unreal (or anti-real). The fantastic world remains closed. It may be only through the inclusion, or omission, of a single piece of information at the beginning of the text, but there will be between author and reader a certain mutual understanding about the level at which everything is to be taken. The assumption, for example, that there are certain people who have the ability to hover in the air, could be the starting-point for a fantastic story of a humorous, uncanny or fairy-tale nature. But as long as the narrative perspective is retained unbroken it will be pure fantasy. Such a story might become *grotesque*, not because of some extraordinary

bizarreness of invention, but because of the alternation or confusion of different perspectives. The hallmark of the grotesque in the realm of the fantastic is the conscious confusion between fantasy and reality.

(p. 37, my trans.)

Mensching pinpoints here a very interesting source of the grotesque: the disorienting and even frightening, but also potentially comic, confusion of the real with the unreal. One has only to look at the relevant paintings by Bosch, Brueghel or, in the twentieth century, surrealists such as Max Ernst and Salvador Dali, to recognize this.

ABNORMALITY

We can get further with the quality of abnormality or unnaturalness (for it is essentially this which, as I have suggested, most earlier commentators meant when they talked of the 'fantastic'). It should be clear that the reaction outlined above as the classic reaction to the grotesque – the experience of amusement and disgust, laughter and horror, mirth and revulsion, simultaneously, is partly at least a reaction to the highly *abnormal*. For the abnormal may be funny (this is accurately reflected in the every-day usage of 'funny' to mean both 'amusing' and 'strange') and on the other hand it may be fearsome or disgusting. Delight in novelty and amusement at a divergence from the normal turns to fear of the unfamiliar and the unknown once a certain degree of abnormality is reached. Mirth at something which fails to conform to accepted standards and norms gives way to fear (and anger) when these norms are seen to be seriously threatened or attacked. This is a paradoxical matter, and we can perhaps make it clearer by taking the example of very small children (good guinea-pigs because their reactions are still spontaneous and uncomplicated) to whom one makes grimaces which increasingly distort the face. The child will laugh at the face pulled only up to a certain point (presumably, while it is still sure of the face as a familiar thing); once this point is passed, once the face becomes so distorted that the child feels threatened, it cries in fear. It is the thin dividing line between the two reactions which is of interest to the student of the grotesque, or, to put it more precisely, the situation where both reactions are evoked at the same time, where both the comic aspect of the abnormal and the fearful or disgusting aspect are felt equally. If we consider the three passages discussed before, we notice in each case a high degree of abnormality in what is being presented, and in each case this abnormality is a source both of the comic and of the disgusting or fearful: most clearly in *Watt*, where we are dealing with actual physical abnormalities, but it is true also for the other passages.

A further example may help to clarify what has been said about abnormality as an essential ingredient of the grotesque. In Smollet's *Humphry Clinker*, we are told of a 'famous Dr L-n' who, upon hearing complaints of the stench caused by river mud, launches 'into a learned investigation of the nature of stink'.

He observed, that stink, or stench, meant no more than a strong impression on the olfactory nerves; and might be applied to substances of the most opposite qualities; that in the Dutch language, stinken signifies the most agreeable perfume, as well as the most fetid odour, . . .

. . . that the French were pleased with the putrid effluvia of animal food; and so were the Hottentots in Africa, and the Savages in Greenland; and that the Negroes on the coast of Senegal would not touch fish till it was rotten; strong presumptions in favour of what is generally called stink, as those nations are in a state of nature undebauched by luxury, unseduced by whim and caprice: that he had reason to believe the stercoraceous flavour, condemned by prejudice as a stink, was, in fact, most agreeable to the organs of smelling: for, that every person who pretended to nauseate the smell of another's execretions, snuffed up his own with particular complacency; for the

c

truth of which he appealed to all the ladies and gentlemen then present: he said, the inhabitants of Madrid and Edinburgh found particular satisfaction in breathing their own atmosphere, which was always impregnated with stercoraceous effluvia: that the learned Dr B-, in his treatise on the Four Digestions, explains in what manner the volatile effluvia from the intestines stimulate and promote the operations of the animal economy; he affirmed, the last Grand Duke of Tuscany, of the Medicis family, who refined upon sensuality with the spirit of a philosopher, was so delighted with that odour that he caused the essence of ordure to be extracted, and used it as the most delicious perfume: that he himself (the doctor) when he happened to be low-spirited, or fatigued with business, found immediate relief and uncommon satisfaction from hanging over the stale contents of a close-stool, while his servant stirred it about under his nose . . .

(Penguin, Harmondsworth, 1967, pp. 45–6)

We may well call this passage extravagant, outlandish and indecent (all epithets commonly used in relation to the grotesque) but, as suggested earlier, we shall understand better the special quality of it and similar passages if we work with the more objective term 'abnormal'. The preposterous doctor and his eccentric ideas are so divergent from the norm that they excite both our laughter and our disgust.

The essentially abnormal nature of the grotesque, and the direct and often radical manner in which this abnormality is presented, is responsible perhaps more than anything else for the not infrequent condemnation of the grotesque as offensive and uncivilized, as an affront to decency and an outrage to 'reality' and 'normality' – or, expressed in the less obviously moralistic language of aesthetic criticism, as tasteless and gratuitous distortion or forced, meaningless exaggeration. People's reaction to the abnormal varies enormously: the conservative man will tend to dismiss it in the above manner, the person who delights in the unusual and the novel will rather be fascinated. This is one reason why one person will find the kind of examples quoted in this book simply nauseating or horrifying, another simply funny, and a third (but I suggest this category is by far the largest) both things at once.

A DEFINITION

The preceding discussion of the role of the abnormal in the grotesque should not be allowed to dominate our notion of the phenomenon as a whole. The abnormal is a secondary factor, of great importance but subsidiary to what I have outlined as the basic definition of the grotesque: *the unresolved clash of incompatibles in work and response*. It is significant that this clash is paralleled by the ambivalent nature of the abnormal as present in the grotesque: we might consider a secondary definition of the grotesque to be '*the ambivalently abnormal*'.

THE SATIRIC AND THE PLAYFUL GROTESQUE

It has been fairly common practice to distinguish several varieties of the grotesque, in particular to set apart the 'satiric-grotesque' from the purely playful, purposeless or ornamental grotesque. This raises the question, to be examined more thoroughly in a later section, of the aims and functions of the grotesque. It is clear that between the employment of the grotesque purely as a weapon of satire and its use as fanciful decoration (as in the original grotesques uncovered around 1500) there is a whole range of possible functions which the grotesque may fulfil. Moreover, it is not always easy to decide what the primary purpose of a piece of grotesquery is: for example, in the passage from *Humphry Clinker* just given, is the grotesque employed solely to ridicule the doctor and his ilk, or do we sense something extra – a dwelling on and savouring of the ludicrous and the nauseating for their own sake, perhaps? On the other hand, is the following passage from Browning's *Caliban upon Setebos*, which Bagehot quotes as an example of the grotesque, mere indulgence in the ludicrously ugly, or is it (given the context of the whole poem) indicative of a profoundly tortured and agonized view of man and nature?

> . . . Will sprawl, now that the heat of day is best,
> Flat on his belly in the pit's much mire,
> With elbows wide, fists clenched to prop his chin.
> And, while he kicks both feet in the cool slush,
> And feels about his spine small eft-things course,
> Run in and out each arm, and make him laugh;
> And while above his head a pompion-plant,
> Coating the cave-top as a brow its eye,
> Creeps down to touch and tickle hair and beard,
> And now a flower drops with a bee inside,
> And now a fruit to snap at, catch and crunch. . .

The other question one asks oneself about this passage is: Is it really grotesque at all? By the criteria we have so far established it seems a very dubious case, and the suspicion is strengthened that what Bagehot, in company with many critics of his time, classed as grotesque, was simply somewhat bizarre and 'vulgar'.

Something more needs to be said at this point about the exaggerated, extreme and radical nature of the grotesque. Critics through the ages have commented on this, some unfavourably (the classical-minded in the main, since a sense of proportion and a measured dignity were values they found overturned by the grotesque) and some with unconcealed delight (Hugo, Chesterton and Bakhtin, notably). It is its radicality which marks the grotesque off from related categories such as the bizarre. Clearly, also, it plays a considerable role in the impact of the grotesque. Further, it should be noted that this radicality exists in both substance and presentation: in the subject-matter presented and in the means employed in the presentation.

4
The Grotesque
and Related Terms and Modes

We have spoken of the grotesque as the unresolved clash of incompatibles, one of which is some form of the comic, and also as the ambivalently abnormal. The first is a rather abstract definition, referring to the pattern or structure fundamental to the grotesque; the second is concerned more with the content of the grotesque. Both, however, are simply different ways of talking about the same thing. It may be of some help at this stage to consider the grotesque in relation to certain other modes and categories, in order first to establish where the dividing lines are and second to see what variations there may be in the basic grotesque pattern outlined so far.

THE ABSURD

'Absurd', like 'grotesque' has suffered from excessive and lax use for some time. Both terms are often applied to something which is merely ridiculous, highly eccentric or stupid. If one insists on the strict meaning of 'absurd' – 'opposed to reason' – it is clear that this will not always fit the grotesque. What complicates matters is that 'the Absurd' has, since Camus, become a term with wide implications, and that the use of the word in 'Theatre of the Absurd' has extended its meaning still further. A. P. Hinchliffe (in his discussion of the absurd in The Critical Idiom series) goes into the matter in detail, but we may note for our purposes that the modern use of 'the absurd' in the context of literature (especially of the drama) brings it very close to the grotesque, so much so that the theatre of the absurd could almost as well be called the 'theatre of the grotesque'. Certainly the plays of Beckett, Ionesco, Adamov, Genet, Pinter and so on are a veritable treasure trove of the grotesque. We should probably be hard put to decide between 'grotesque' and 'absurd' to describe such characters as Lucky and Pozzo in *Waiting for Godot*, the Orator in Ionesco's *The Chairs*, and Madame in Genet's *The Maids*, or to characterize scenes like the emergence of Nagg and Nell from their ashbins in Beckett's *Endgame* or the brain-washing episode in Act II of Pinter's *The Birthday Party*, where Stanley is interrogated by Goldberg and McCann:

> *Goldberg:* Do you recognize an external force?
> *Stanley:* What?
> *Goldberg:* Do you recognize an external force?
> *McCann:* That's the question!
> *Goldberg:* Do you recognize an external force, responsible for you, suffering for you?
> *Stanley:* It's late.
> *Goldberg:* Late! Late enough! When did you last pray?
> *McCann:* He's sweating!
> *Goldberg:* When did you last pray?
> *McCann:* He's sweating!
> *Goldberg:* Is the number 846 possible or necessary?
> *Stanley:* Neither.
> *Goldberg:* Wrong! Is the number 846 possible or necessary?
> *Stanley:* Both.
> *Goldberg:* Wrong! It's necessary but not possible.
> *Stanley:* Both.
> *Goldberg:* Wrong! Why do you think the number 846 is necessarily possible?
> *Stanley:* Must be.
> *Goldberg:* Wrong! It's only necessarily necessary! We admit possibility only after we grant necessity. It is possible because necessary but by no means necessary through possibility. The possibility can only be assumed after the proof of necessity.

McCann: Right!

Goldberg: Right? Of course right! We're right and you're wrong, Webber, all along the line.

McCann: All along the line!

Goldberg: Where is your lechery leading you?

McCann: You'll pay for this.

Goldberg: You stuff yourself with dry toast.

McCann: You contaminate womankind.

Goldberg: Why don't you pay the rent?

McCann: Mother defiler!

Goldberg: Why do you pick your nose?

McCann: I demand justice!

Goldberg: What's your trade?

McCann: What about Ireland?

Goldberg: What's your trade?

Stanley: I play the piano.

Goldberg: How many fingers do you use?

Stanley: No hands!

Goldberg: No society would touch you. Not even a building society.

McCann: You're a traitor to the cloth.

Goldberg: What do you use for pyjamas?

Stanley: Nothing.

Goldberg: You verminate the sheet of your birth.

McCann: What about the Albigensenist heresy?

Goldberg: Who watered the wicket in Melbourne?

McCann: What about the blessed Oliver Plunkett?

Goldberg: Speak up Webber. Why did the chicken cross the road?

Stanley: He wanted to – he wanted to – he wanted to . . .

McCann: He doesn't know!

Goldberg: Why did the chicken cross the road?

But the choice between 'absurd' and 'grotesque' for such scenes represents a false alternative, for there is no reason why all of these should not be absurd (in the sense in which the word is currently applied) and grotesque at the same time. There is, however, a crucial difference between the two terms. We have seen that the grotesque can be reduced to a certain formal pattern. But there is no formal pattern, no structural characteristics peculiar to the absurd: it can only be perceived as content, as a quality, a feeling or atmosphere, an attitude or world-view. The formal means of presenting it are many and varied: the absurd can be expressed through irony, or through philosophic argument, or through the grotesque itself. In connection with the latter possibility, we should note that consistent perception of the grotesque, or the perception of grotesqueness on a grand scale, can lead to the notion of universal absurdity.

THE BIZARRE

The difference between the bizarre and the grotesque is mainly one of degree. The grotesque is more radical and usually more aggressive. Kayser expresses the difference by calling the grotesque more dangerous: the bizarre, he points out, can be used synonymously with 'very strange', 'outlandish' – it lacks the disturbing quality of the grotesque. Here one again of course runs into the problem of subjectivity: what is grotesque to one person may be only bizarre to another. But the difference in degree, as a statement of principle, is none the less valid, and Kayser's point is surely a good one. We are unlikely to find anything very disturbing in the following poem by Robert Graves:

> Dr Newman with the crooked pince-nez
> Had studied in Vienna and Chicago.
> Chess was his only relaxation.
> And Dr Newman remained unperturbed
> By every nastier manifestation
> Of pluto-democratic civilization;
> All that was cranky, corny, ill-behaved,
> Unnecessary, askew or orgiastic
> Would creep unbidden to his side-door (hidden
> Behind a poster in the Tube Station,

Nearly half-way up the moving stairs),
Push its way in, to squat there undisturbed
Among box-files and tubular steel-chairs.

He was once seen at the Philharmonic Hall
Noting the reactions of two patients,
With pronounced paranoiac tendencies,
To old Dutch music. He appeared to recall
A tin of lozenges in his breast-pocket,
Put his hand confidently in —
And drew out a black imp, or sooterkin,
Six inches long, with one ear upside-down,
Licking at a vanilla ice-cream cornet —
Then put it back again with a slight frown.

Most people, I think, would call this bizarre, not grotesque. But –
just to illustrate how one man's bizarre can be another man's
grotesque – this is one of six poems which Graves groups under
the general title 'Grotesques'. Of course, the dividing line may in
any case be very difficult to draw, and one can point to a number
of works where the bizarre turns into the grotesque for a brief
moment. We can describe this process in technical terms in the
following way: something which is very strange, and perhaps
ludicrous as well, is made so exceedingly abnormal that our
laughter at the ludicrous and eccentric is intruded on by feelings of
horror or disgust; or, a scene or character which is laughably
eccentric suddenly becomes problematic, and our reaction to it
mixed, through the appearance of something quite at odds with the
comic. We may observe this phenomenon in an example from
Tristram Shandy:

That this *Ambrose Paroeus* was chief surgeon and nose-mender to
Francis the ninth of *France*, and in high credit with him and the two
preceding, or succeeding kings (I know not which) – and that, except
in the slip he made in his story of *Taliacotius's* noses, and his manner
of setting them on – he was esteemed by the whole college of

physicians at that time, as more knowing in matters of noses, than anyone who had ever taken them in hand.

Now *Ambrose Paroeus* convinced my father, that the true and efficient cause of what had engaged so much the attention of the world, and upon which *Prignitz* and *Scroderus* had wasted so much learning and fine parts – was neither this nor that – but that the length and goodness of the nose was owing simply to the softness and flaccidity in the nurse's breast – as the flatness and shortness of *puisne* noses was to the firmness and elastic repulsion of the same organ of nutrition in the hale and lively – which, tho' happy for the woman, was the undoing of the child, inasmuch as his nose was so snubb'd, so rebuff'd, so rebated, and so refrigerated thereby, as never to arrive *ad mensuram suam legitimam*, – but that in case of the flaccidity and softness of the nurse or mother's breast – by sinking into it, quoth *Paroeus*, as into so much butter, the nose was comforted, nourish'd, plump'd up, refresh'd, refocillated, and set a growing for ever.

I have but two things to observe of Paroeus; first, That he proves and explains all this with the utmost chastity and decorum of expression – for which may his soul for ever rest in peace! . . .

(Everyman edition, London, 1956, pp. 169–70)

What begins as a merely eccentric and bizarre account of a theory of nose shapes and sizes becomes perhaps somewhat disturbing with the mention of the infant nose sinking into the breast 'as into so much butter'. It would be too much to say that this image is monstrous, but there is something unsettling about the confusion between animate and inanimate, between the female breast and a lump of butter (perhaps the association of butter with milk, in the context, adds to this), and about the suggestion that the nose actually feeds upon the breast. But the feeling is there only for a moment; instead of developing the image further in the direction of grotesquery, as he doubtless could have, Sterne – and this is typical of him – returns to his whimsical style, with assurances that Paroeus expounds his theory 'with the utmost chastity and decorum of expression'.

Two further things are worth noting in passing about this

passage. The first is that any writer whose natural element, so to speak, is the whimsical, the slightly off-key and eccentric, almost inevitably drops into the grotesque mode from time to time. (Diderot is another who immediately comes to mind: *Le neveu de Rameau* and *Jacques le fataliste* both present wonderfully eccentric – and occasionally grotesque – characters.) Once again, the dividing lines are difficult to draw, and there are many who regard these works of Sterne and Diderot as grotesque not only in places but through and through.

Second, the confusion between animate and inanimate referred to above recalls an important feature of the original grotesque paintings described by Vitruvius and imitated by Renaissance painters: the interweaving of plant, animal, human and architectural forms, so that a stone pedestal would become the torso of a human figure with curling plants for arms and an animal's head. It also brings to mind those theories of the comic, principally Henri Bergson's in *Le rire*, which attempt to locate the source of laughter in the perception of living things, especially human beings, as inanimate, and conversely also in the perception of inanimate objects as alive. Bergson's is a rather narrow and one-sided definition of the comic, and Kayser is closer to the mark when he classes this kind of confusion as one of the basic *grotesque* techniques, and mentions in this connection the puppet or marionette. Certainly there is something potentially grotesque about marionettes, automatons and the like. Human-like, animated yet actually lifeless objects, they are apt to be simultaneously comical and eerie – comical because of their imperfect approximation to human form and behaviour, eerie probably because of age-old, deep-rooted fears in man of animated and human-like objects. Conversely, a human being giving the appearance of being a marionette or robot is likewise grotesque: comical and strangely disturbing at the same time. Hence also the common description of dead bodies: 'The body lay in a grotesque position' – i.e. in a position normally only assumable by marionettes and dolls, with limbs and head in unnatural positions.

THE MACABRE

It should be clear from what has been said so far that the macabre and the grotesque frequently overlap. One would have difficulty, for example, in deciding on the one or the other term to describe the following death scene from Günter Grass's novel *The Tin Drum*. The dwarf hero Oskar, surrounded, together with his parents, by Russian soldiers in a cellar, hands back to his father Matzerath the latter's Nazi party pin:

> Anyway, he grasped. I was rid of the thing. Little by little, fear took possession of Matzerath as he felt the emblem of his Party between his fingers. Now that my hands were free, I didn't want to see what Matzerath did with the pin. Too distraught to pursue the lice, Oskar tried to concentrate on the ants, but couldn't help taking in a swift movement of Matzerath's hand. Unable to remember what I thought at the time, I can only say in retrospect that it would have been wiser of him to keep the little coloured lozenge in his hand.
>
> But he wanted desperately to get rid of it, and despite the rich imagination he had shown as a cook and window dresser, he could think of no other hiding place than his mouth.
>
> How important a trifling gesture can be! That little move from hand to mouth was enough to startle the two Ivans who had been sitting peacefully to left and right of Maria and make them jump up from the air-defence cot. They thrust their tommy guns at Matzerath's belly, and it was plain for all to see that Matzerath was trying to swallow something.
>
> If only he had first, with an adroit finger manœuvre, closed the pin. As it was, he gagged, his face went purple, his eyes stood out of his head, he coughed, cried, laughed, and all this turmoil made it impossible for him to keep his hands up. But on that point the Ivans were firm. They shouted at him, they wanted to see the palms of his hands. Matzerath, however, was preoccupied with his windpipe. He

couldn't even cough properly. He began to dance and thrash about with his arms and swept a can of Leipzig stew off the shelf. My Kalmuck, who until then had been quietly looking on, deposited me carefully on the floor, reached behind him, brought something or other into a horizontal position, and shot from the hip. He had emptied a whole magazine before Matzerath finished suffocating.

(trans. by Ralph Manheim, Penguin, Harmondsworth, 1965, pp. 386–7)

This, like so many other passages in the novel, is prevented from being simply horrifying (but at the same time, paradoxically, made *more* ghastly) by several things which cut across the horror. Apart from the ironic implications of Matzerath's swallowing the party pin (in the associations with 'swallowing the evidence' and 'his shame choking him') there are numerous touches which introduce a comic element which is utterly at odds with the horror of the scene: touches such as '... despite the rich imagination he had shown as a cook and window dresser' and particularly the sentence 'He began to dance and thrash about with his arms and swept a can of Leipzig stew off the shelf'.

But is this macabre rather than grotesque? One might well want to answer that it is both, and that the macabre, if one understands it as the horrifying tinged with the comic, is a sub-form of the grotesque. Strictly speaking, macabre means 'pertaining to death' and it is only in comparatively recent usage that it has developed the connotation 'gruesome yet funny' (through association with 'macabre humour', 'macabre joke'). And it is still true that the gruesome element in the macabre considerably outweighs the comic. Often the latter represents not a confusing quality but a heightening of the horrible or gruesome: that is, the strange comic tinge is used to increase sensitivity to gruesomeness which, presented unadulterated in large doses, may dull our responses. In any case, the macabre seems to lack the balanced tension between opposites which is a feature of the grotesque. But this may be splitting hairs. What is one to do with, for example, the protracted murder scene at the end of Nabokov's *Lolita*?

CARICATURE

The grotesque has always been strongly associated with caricature, and even placed in the same category by some theorists, notably those who saw simple distortion as the basic principle in grotesque art. Caricature may be briefly defined as the ludicrous exaggeration of characteristic or peculiar features. A major distinction from the grotesque as we have sought to describe it at once becomes clear: in caricature there need be no suggestion of the *confusion* of heterogeneous and incompatible elements, no sense of the intrusion of alien elements. The difference can be felt plainly in one's reaction. One laughs at a caricature because a recognizable or typical person or characteristic is distorted (or stylized) in a ridiculous and amusing way – that is, a peculiar feature is exaggerated to the point of abnormality. It is a straightforward, uncomplicated reaction to something which has a straightforward function and clearly discernible intention, whereas one's reaction to the grotesque is essentially divided and problematic. It only becomes difficult to distinguish between caricature and the grotesque (and then the distinction is academic) when the caricaturistic exaggeration becomes extreme or develops into exaggeration for its own sake. Thus a sketch of the late General de Gaulle in which the nose is made disproportionately large would be a caricature; but if one increasingly exaggerates the size of the nose until the point is reached where it appears that the rest of the face is entirely subservient to and controlled by the nose (the tail wagging the dog, as it were), then this is likely to be a grotesque caricature. Not only has the normal relationship of face to nose been reversed but the nose has taken on an almost autonomous quality and so to speak assumed a separate existence. In other words there is a norm for caricaturistic exaggeration – a norm of abnormality. When this norm is exceeded, the caricature is no longer simply funny, but disgusting or fearsome besides, for it approaches the realm of the monstrous. Many of the caricatures of Daumier, Grandville or of George Grosz are of this kind.

In literature particularly it is not just the degree of distortion or exaggeration which determines whether we find the caricature simply funny or disgusting besides. Obviously, the manner in which the caricatured person or feature is presented is a further important factor. Thus Shakespeare's Sir Andrew Aguecheek strikes us simply as ridiculous and comic; the fop is not seen as threatening or disgusting, he is harmless. Malvolio on the other hand may well appear grotesque, at least on occasions, because he is not only ridiculous, but presented also as being malevolent. Clayborough has attempted to show that a number of Dickens's characters with pronounced caricaturistic features (Clayborough calls them 'eccentric' characters) are grotesque. While harbouring serious doubts about the broadness of his application of 'grotesque' one can see clearly that many of Dickens's figures – Clayborough mentions Mrs Gamp, Fagin, Uriah Heep, Quilp, Mr Micawber and several others – are at least on some occasions grotesque. One character not mentioned by Clayborough is Mrs Pipchin from *Dombey and Son*, who is described as follows:

This celebrated Mrs Pipchin was a marvellous ill-favoured, ill-conditioned old lady, of a stooping figure, with a mottled face, like bad marble, a hook nose, and a hard grey eye, that looked as if it might have been hammered at on an anvil without sustaining any injury. Forty years at least had elapsed since the Peruvian mines had been the death of Mr Pipchin; but his relict still wore black bombazeen, of such a lustreless, deep, dead, sombre shade, that gas itself couldn't light her up after dark, and her presence was a quencher to any number of candles. . . . She was such a bitter old lady, that one was tempted to believe there had been some mistake in the application of the Peruvian machinery, and that all her waters of gladness and milk of human kindness, had been pumped out dry, instead of the mines.

(Penguin, Harmondsworth, 1970, p. 160)

If Mrs Pipchin is a grotesque caricature, her parlour is likewise grotesquely reminiscent of some monster's abode:

It was not, naturally, a fresh-smelling house; and in the window of the front parlour, which was never opened, Mrs Pipchin kept a collection of plants in pots, which imparted an earthy flavour of their own to the establishment. However choice examples of their kind, too, these plants were of a kind peculiarly adapted to the embowerment of Mrs Pipchin. There were half a dozen specimens of the cactus, writhing round bits of lath, like hairy serpents; another specimen shooting out broad claws, like a green lobster; several creeping vegetables, possessed of sticky and adhesive leaves; and one uncomfortable flower-pot hanging to the ceiling, which appeared to have boiled over, and tickling people underneath with its long green ends, reminded them of spiders – in which Mrs Pipchin's dwelling was uncommonly prolific, though perhaps it challenged competition still more proudly, in the season, in point of earwigs.

(ibid., pp. 160–1)

PARODY

Parody is often involved with the grotesque in an interdependent relationship of which it can be difficult to determine whether it is a case of parody being used as a grotesque device or vice versa. A parody (or travesty, or burlesque – for our present purposes we may lump them together) which is taken to extremes, that is to a point where the conflict between parody and original, or between content and form, becomes intolerable – we might call a grotesque parody, and the grotesqueness may even blot out the parodistic intent. Similarly, grotesque elements are frequently used incidentally in parodies, especially where the intention is savagely aggressive. On the other hand, parody is a favourite device of the grotesque writer. But here again the relationship is that between the essential and the incidental: parody is used occasionally, to help achieve an overall grotesque effect. Bert Brecht's poem 'Legend of the Dead Soldier' is a good example of this interdependent relationship between parody and the grotesque. It is a poem in conventional ballad form, relating the wondrous 'legend' of a soldier in the First World War. He has been killed, but, since the Kaiser needs more men, is dug up from his grave and brought back to life, ministered to by a nursing sister and a cleric, supported by two medical attendants, has his stinking remains dressed in the German flag (a superbly grotesque touch) and is finally led in triumphant procession, cheered on by the local populace, back to the front. The term one would want to use to best describe the nature of the poem would be grotesque satire (of which more later), but parody is used throughout in a supporting role. Thus the ludicrous contrast between the traditional ballad form, conventionally used for stirring tales of adventure, and the actual horrifying and sordid content is heightened by numerous parodistic touches which are all at the same time grotesque. The ballad as a conventional genre very much associated with patriotic themes is by this process dragged in the mud, made to look grotesquely inappropriate, while Brecht's merciless satire on the war-machine and its insatiable need for more cannon-fodder is also highlighted by some memorable pieces of grotesquery.

SATIRE

The same kind of interdependent relationship is found often between satire and the grotesque. The satirist may make his victim grotesque in order to produce in his audience or readers a maximum reaction of derisive laughter and disgust; and a grotesque text, on the other hand, will frequently have a satirical side-effect or score satirical points, naturally enough when one considers that the grotesque by its very nature is aggressive and aimed at discomfiting in some way. But again the crucial factor separating the grotesque from satire is the *confusion* of incompatibles in work and effect. Unlike the satirist, the grotesque writer does not analyse and instruct in terms of right and wrong, or true or false, nor does he attempt to distinguish between these. On the contrary, he is concerned to demonstrate their inseparability. Satire (and we are of course talking about model cases) aims at two reactions from the audience: laughter, and anger or disgust, but it aims to produce these separately. The grotesque, as we have seen repeatedly, produces a confusion of reaction. Normally in satire there is an alternation, or at least a distinction, between the ludicrous smallness which excites derisive laughter and the gross evil which arouses anger. The grotesque writer would present ludicrous smallness and gross evil as being one, indistinguishable, and strive for a reaction in which laughter and anger figure simultaneously and with equal force.

The above distinction between the grotesque and satire has been made somewhat baldly for the purpose of clarity, but it should be clear that the satirist who uses the grotesque as a tool, a shock-weapon, must be careful. There is a danger that the didactic point he wishes to make may be obscured for the reader by the nonplussing, disorienting and generally overwhelming effect of the grotesque. The grotesque is in this sense *anti-rational* and not conducive to the grasping of satiric points. Should it be used indiscriminately it is apt to dominate the attention of the reader and possibly confuse him. Heinrich Schneegans, referring principally to Rabelais, has described this tendency of the grotesque to 'take over' a text:

> The grotesque satirist exaggerates at first only for satiric purposes. But it is in the nature of this kind of powerful, extreme satire that its exaggerations burst through all limits. The grotesque satirist becomes intoxicated with his own creation. Gradually he loses sight of the

satire. The exaggerations which he had at first unleashed in full awareness of their purpose become more and more wild, until they get out of hand, obliterating like a turbulent stream everything around them.

(*Geschichte der grotesken Satire*, p. 248, my trans.)

It would require a long example to properly illustrate this process, but the passage from *Humphry Clinker* quoted above (pp. 25–6) may be a case of it, and readers of Rabelais will doubtless recall innumerable instances where a scene which begins in a straight-forwardly satiric fashion rapidly develops into a wild romp – one can sense Rabelais delightedly creating more and more fantastic and outlandish complications – until very soon the original point is lost from view. The following extract from a poem by Swift may also illustrate this tendency of the grotesque to take over our attention.

A Beautiful Young Nymph Going to Bed

Corinna, pride of Drury Lane,
For whom no shepherd sighs in vain;
Never did Covent Garden boast
So bright a batter'd strolling toast!
No drunken rake to pick her up,
No cellar where on tick to sup;
Returning at the midnight hour,
Four stories climbing to her bower;
Then, seated on a three-legg'd chair,
Takes off her artificial hair;
Now picking out a crystal eye,
She wipes it clean, and lays it by.
Her eyebrows from a mouse's hide
Stuck on with art on either side,
Pulls off with care, and first displays 'em
Then in a play-book smoothly lays 'em.
Now dextrously her plumpers draws,
That serve to fill her hollow jaws,

Untwists a wire, and from her gums
A set of teeth completely comes;
Pulls out the rags contrived to prop
Her flabby dugs, and down they drop.
Proceeding on, the lovely goddess
Unlaces next her steel-ribb'd bodice,
Which, by the operator's skill,
Press down the lumps, the hollows fill.
Up goes her hand, and off she slips
The bolsters that supply her hips;
With gentlest touch she next explores
Her chancres, issues, running sores;
Effects of many a sad disaster,
And then to each applies a plaster:
But must, before she goes to bed,
Rub off the daubs of white and red,
And smooth the furrows in her front
With greasy paper stuck upon't.
She takes a bolus ere she sleeps ...

Swift's exposure is so savage, his desire to wound, disgust and deride so powerful, that, paradoxically, we are apt to respond more to the grotesqueness of his description than to the point he is making. What remains most clearly in one's mind after finishing the poem is not the insight into the true nature of apparently beautiful maidens but the overwhelming impression of the grotesqueness of the details. Of course, in this case where the satire is uncomplicated we can readily, at least on a moment's reflection, penetrate to Swift's 'message'; but where satire is at all complex and subtle, the grotesque can be a disruptive and distracting force. In Rabelais, this usually takes the form of the genuinely satiric being abandoned in favour of the grotesquely bawdy or scurrilous. Thus one of the many send-ups of learned medical discourses, the discussion in Book 1, Chapter 13 of *Gargantua and Pantagruel* on methods of – to use a very un-Rabelaisian euphemism – anal cleanliness, very quickly loses any point beyond the monstrous and comic invention of more and more unlikely methods; and in the episode described in Book 2, Chapters 21 and 22 concerning the Parisian lady to whom Panurge takes a fancy Rabelais hardly pursues the satiric point regarding the lady's (apparent) virtue at all, preferring once again to indulge his liking for the obscene and grotesque, having Panurge sprinkle the unfortunate woman's garments with the ground-up pudendum of a bitch on heat, with the following outrageous results:

> Panurge had no sooner spoken than all the dogs in the church ran up to the lady, attracted by the smell he had sprinkled on her. Small and great, big and little, all came, lifting their legs, smelling her and pissing all over her. It was the most dreadful thing in the world.
>
> Panurge made a show of driving them off, then took leave of her and retired into a chapel to see the fun. For these beastly dogs pissed over all her clothes, a great greyhound wetting her on the head, others on her sleeves, others on her backside; and the little ones pissed on her shoes; so that all the women who were thereabouts had great difficulty in saving her.
>
> At this Panurge burst out laughing, and said to some of the gentlemen of the city: 'I think that woman's on heat, or else she has recently been covered by a greyhound.'
>
> (trans. by J. M. Cohen, Penguin, Harmondsworth, 1963, pp. 243–4)

The implications of the term 'the satiric-grotesque' are thus not so simple as many critics who employ it seem to consider. If I have perhaps overstressed the potentially disruptive nature of the grotesque in the preceding discussion, it was only to make clear some of the problems associated with the use of the grotesque as a satiric weapon, and to point out that, while the grotesque is often found in satiric literature, one does well to remember its essential distinctness. It is of course clear that clever satirists – Swift himself figures large among them – are able to extract a maximum of effect from their use of the grotesque without in any way diminishing the strength of the overall satiric point they wish to make. Evelyn

Waugh's *The Loved One* provides numerous examples of the successful harnessing of the grotesque to a satiric purpose. Here is the hero making arrangements to have a 'Loved One' prepared for 'leave-taking' in Whispering Glades:

'Let us now decide on the casket.'

They went to the show-rooms where stood coffins of every shape and material: the nightingale still sang in the cornice.

'The two-piece lid is most popular for gentlemen Loved Ones. Only the upper part is then exposed to view.'

'Exposed to view?'

'Yes, when the Waiting Ones come to take leave.'

'But I say, I don't think that will quite do. I've seen him. He's terribly disfigured, you know.'

'If there are any special little difficulties in the case you must mention them to our cosmeticians. You will be seeing one of them before you leave. They have never failed yet.'

'We had a Loved One last month who was found drowned. He had been in the ocean a month and they only identified him by his wrist-watch. They fixed that stiff,' said the hostess disconcertingly lapsing from the high diction she had hitherto employed, 'so he looked like it was his wedding day. The boys up there surely know their job. Why, if he'd sat on an atom bomb, they'd make him presentable.'

'That's very comforting.'

'I'll say it is.' And then slipping on her professional manner again as though it were a pair of glasses, she resumed.

'How will the Loved One be attired? We have our own tailoring section. Sometimes after a very long illness there are not suitable clothes available and sometimes the Waiting Ones think it a waste of a good suit. You see, we can fit a Loved One out very reasonably as a casket-suit does not have to be designed for hard wear and in cases where only the upper part is exposed for leave-taking there is no need for more than jacket and vest. Something dark is best to set off the flowers.'

(Penguin, Harmondsworth, 1969, pp. 39–40)

Waugh manages here to achieve his satiric aim – the exposure and comic deflation of the Californian 'way of death' with all its euphemistic vulgarity – with devastating effect, because what is grotesque is his target itself: Whispering Glades, its staff and its customs are all simultaneously comic and ghastly. Waugh brings out both aspects to the full, but never so that his satiric point is obscured.

IRONY

Some aspects of the relationship between the grotesque and irony have been touched upon. It is clear that, like the satirist, the ironist too may very well reach for the grotesque as a weapon from time to time. But, again like the satirist, he must use it judiciously or he may find that it takes over and the irony goes by the board. Irony is primarily intellectual in its function and appeal, and the grotesque primarily emotional. This is somewhat baldly stated, but essentially true nevertheless. The impact of the grotesque is characteristically one of a sudden shock, which is likely to stun, bewilder or nonplus – the mind takes a few seconds to function dispassionately again. Irony, on the other hand, depends very much for its effect on the reader's being given the chance intellectually to make distinctions and connections. In the extreme case, the grotesque writer will deliberately prevent a rational and intellectual approach to his work, demonstrating that the intolerable and inextricable mixture of incompatibles is a fact of life, perhaps the most crucial one. The ironist places the incompatibles also in some kind of relationship, but it is always a relationship which can be 'worked out'. Much of one's pleasure in irony comes after all from detecting it.

Having said this it is necessary – as was the case with satire – to add that dividing-lines are uncertain and relationships shifting. Clearly, there is such a thing as grotesque irony. Swift's *Modest Proposal* is an example of this. The piece on the whole is satire through irony – common enough – but it is irony of a particularly savage kind. So savage, in fact, so extreme and so radically presented, that it is inevitably very close to the grotesque. And certain parts of the tract are undoubtedly, taken by themselves, grotesque. One has been quoted earlier – in particular the initial disclosure of just what the proposal entails is monstrously grotesque:

> I have been assured by a very knowing American of my Acquaintance in London; that a young healthy Child, well nursed, is at a Year old, a most delicious, nourishing, and wholesome Food; whether Stewed, Roasted, Baked or Boiled: and, I make no doubt, that it will equally serve in a Fricasie, or Ragoust.

Up to this point the reader has been intellectually regaled by Swift's irony and made morally indignant by the point of it: the exposure of the inhuman conditions in Ireland. These two responses have not, however, constituted a conflict. As with all satire – and this is satire, by means of irony – one can experience amusement and delight at the cleverness of the exposure at the same time as indignation at the evil thus uncovered, without feeling these to be in any way contradictory. Swift's role as the efficiency-minded economist, earnestly setting out the problem to be solved in careful statistical terms, is amusing because we see that it is a parody of those dry impersonal schemes for dealing with pitiable human problems, and didactically effective because the inhumanity of such schemes and their authors is thus exposed. But when this role leads to the advancement of cannibalism as an economic remedy, amusement at the cleverness and appreciation of the direction of attack are suddenly joined by a third response, horror, which conflicts with them. It is essentially the element of exaggeration, the sudden radicalizing, which is the crucial factor in this. Although we know that the 'I' of the tract is a fictitious, assumed one, a persona or role, and that Swift is being ironic, the sheer enormity of the proposal for cannibalism horrifies us, so that, for a moment, we are uncertain of our response, uncertain of how we are to take this. It may even be that at this moment our knowledge that the 'I' is an ironic device is submerged, or suspended, and we react in a way as though the proposal were being put seriously, so powerful is its brutality and so sudden its announcement. A powerful emotional impact has been created, conflicting with the standard response to irony. This accords entirely with Swift's purpose: the proposal serves to jolt the reader, alarm and horrify him with a sudden reminder that this is no joking matter. It is a common enough Swiftian technique: he screws the irony and satire tighter and tighter till a point is reached where one's laughter becomes mixed with revulsion and horror. Once a certain degree of exaggeration – or radicality – has been reached we find ourselves confronted with irony that has become grotesque. It is only the continual inclusion of pointers to the ironic nature of the whole that prevents the grotesque from 'getting out of hand', to use Kayser's phrase, and obliterating the point. In this sense we must see *A Modest Proposal* as an example (and a very fine example) of the grotesque used within an ironic-satiric framework: among the blows in Swift's repertoire, the grotesque supplies the belly-punches.

Swift's tract contains of course basically only one type of irony, though it is the kind which most often displays affinities with the grotesque. Apart from this, the type of irony usually referred to as cosmic or universal is the most likely to become grotesque. A world-view based on the notion of infinite irony (A is ironized by B is ironized by C, and so on *ad infinitum*) or of mutual irony on a grand scale (we perceive that A is ironized by B, but the presence of a third factor C might well reverse this, and so on), necessarily implies also notions of universal grotesqueness and universal absurdity. At this level the distinction between irony, the grotesque and the absurd becomes a rather pedantic distinction between different aspects of chaos.

On the whole, however, what was earlier established as the crucial distinction between irony and the grotesque holds true: irony depends on the resolvability, intellectually, of a relationship (appearance/reality, truth/untruth, etc.), while the grotesque presents essentially the unresolvability of incompatibles. Generally, it is not difficult to separate irony and the grotesque unless the irony is particularly strong and unexpected – in other words, unless a high degree of exaggeration or radicality, and the concomitant emotional shock, however short-lived, are involved. A monstrously ironic situation or statement may be felt to be grotesque because of the sheer enormity of it. Much of the irony in Kafka is of this kind.

THE COMIC

The relationship of the grotesque to the comic is a matter of some controversy. As mentioned earlier, modern writers on the grotesque are almost unanimous in their insistence on the essential comic element in the grotesque. An exception may be Clayborough, but since he operates with different categories (Jungian) it is difficult to see just where he stands on the comic. Kayser is likewise evasive, but seems in the end to accept the necessary presence of the comic in the grotesque. In the present study I have taken the view that there is almost always a comic element in the grotesque (although it may be obscured and in some circumstances denied by rational afterthought). This accords with the historical development of the term, with the majority of modern commentators and with everyday usage. The latter is often a dubious guide where aesthetic terms are concerned, but it is interesting that 'grotesque' in everyday speech usually refers to something which the speaker finds simultaneously funny and repulsive, be it a politician's speech, an extremely bad production of a play, a public scandal or a piece of interior decoration. If the epithet 'grotesque' is used then the politician's speech does not simply provoke the anger or contempt of the person concerned, but arouses also his sense of the ludicrous; the bad production is so bad that it is not just appalling but comic; the indignation one feels at the scandal is mingled with an appreciation of its farcical nature; the interior decoration is nauseating because of its tastelessness but at the same time comic because of its ineptitude. It is significant too that the word is only used in reference to extreme situations and events. One has recourse to it when 'appalling', 'disgusting' etc. are not powerful enough or do not cover the extra quality perceived: this extra quality being the comic, in opposition to and in conflict with something incompatible with it.

It may perhaps be objected that the insistence on the comic as, so to speak, one half of the grotesque unnecessarily narrows the term, and that it is enough to speak of the paradox of attraction/repulsion to characterize the conflict which is basic to the grotesque. Certainly this paradox may be felt in many, perhaps all, instances of the grotesque, but as a defining factor it is surely inadequate. One needs to dig deeper and specify what may constitute the attraction and what the repulsion. And it is difficult to go past the comic as the source of attraction. If one tries to substitute, for example, something like the *fascinating* one will find, I suggest, that actually the fascination which the grotesque has about it is itself usually traceable to the peculiar mixture of the comic with something quite un-comic. One can test this on suitable passages from the kind of uncanny tales associated with Edgar Allan Poe and E. T. A. Hoffman, those tales of the weird and the supernatural which are strangely disturbing. In Hoffmann's *The Sandman*, for example, there are numerous passages which one feels are grotesque but which, one might say, have no comic content at all. But let us have a closer look at one such passage. Nathanael has fallen in love with an automaton, by name Olimpia, constructed by Professor Spalanzani, and marvels at her perfect beauty and evenness of temperament. Entering Spalanzani's house one day, he hears a fearful hubbub coming from the study:

> Nathanael rushed in, impelled by some nameless dread. The Professor was grasping a female figure by the shoulders, the Italian Coppola held her by the feet; and they were pulling and dragging each other backwards and forwards, fighting furiously to get possession of her.
>
> Nathanael recoiled with horror on recognizing that the figure was Olimpia. Boiling with rage, he was about to tear his beloved from the grasp of the madmen, when Coppola by an extraordinary exertion of strength twisted the figure out of the Professor's hands and gave him such a terrible blow with her, that Spalanzani reeled backwards and fell over the table among the phials and retorts, the bottles and glass cylinders, which covered it: all these things were smashed into a thousand pieces. But Coppola threw the figure across his shoulder, and, laughing shrilly and horribly, ran hastily down the stairs, the figure's ugly feet hanging down and banging and rattling like wood against the steps.
>
> Nathanael was stupefied – he had seen only too distinctly that in Olimpia's pallid waxed face there were no eyes, merely black holes in their stead; she was an inanimate puppet.

Even though one has realized by this stage of the tale that Olimpia is in fact an automaton, the scene of two men indulging in a tug of war with a human-like figure, and particularly of Coppola (with his associations with the fairy-tale sandman) lugging this figure down the stairs with its feet clattering against the steps, is disconcerting, perhaps even frightening if one enters into Nathanael's view of things. But it is surely also irresistibly comic, not least because of the slapstick nature of the brawl. I would go further and suggest that, in so far as Nathanael's collapse into madness, which occurs immediately after this scene and again at the end of the tale, is felt to be grotesque, it is because one's sense of the comic is aroused as well as a feeling of horror and pity. Manifestations of insanity, particularly those involving maniacal laughter, are often grotesque, because insane behaviour is abnormal in the particular way spoken of earlier: it can be comic and frightening or pitiable at the same time. G. Wilson Knight, in a well-known essay from *The Wheel of Fire* entitled '*King Lear* and the Comedy of the Grotesque', refers to Lear's madness in these terms, and points out that the impact of the play would be considerably less without the cruel, grim comedy which accompanies the tragic action.

Yet while we may be fairly certain that somewhere in all examples of the grotesque there is a comic element, there are cases which seem to prevent a completely valid generalization. In C. S. Lewis's *That Hideous Strength*, there is a brief description of a painting:

> There was a portrait of a young woman who held her mouth wide open to reveal the fact that the inside of it was thickly overgrown with hair. It was very skilfully painted in the photographic manner so that you could feel that hair.

I think most people would call this grotesque, but is there a comic element here – if not in the description, then in the painting imagined visually? We are on shifting ground here, for the answer one tends to get to questions like this is: 'Well, it depends on . . .' We should perhaps attempt at this stage to clarify the nature of laughter, in so far as it is present, as a reaction to the grotesque. Theories of the comic and of laughter are legion, and the subject has become the concern, not just of aestheticians and philosophers, but, since Freud's study *The Joke and its Relationship to the Unconscious* (1905), also of psychologists. The matter is complicated, in the case of the grotesque, by the presence of one cause of laughter which one might not admit to be connected with the comic. This is the purely defensive laughter with which a person seeks to ward off emotional shock or distress. In its extreme form, this sort of laughter takes on overtones of hysteria; but even in a milder form, the nervous laugh, it cannot be properly seen as a reaction to the *comic*. Laughter purely in defence means that the person concerned does *not* find anything comic in whatever causes it. Whether his reaction is a conscious attempt to 'laugh off' something which distresses him extremely, or whether it is an involuntary physiological reaction need not concern us. We must merely insist that one laughs 'naturally' at the grotesque because one perceives the comic element in it. But even this kind of laughter is not 'free' or undisturbed; the simultaneous perception of the other side of the grotesque – its horrifying, disgusting or frightening aspect – confuses the reaction. Thus one may well laugh at the grotesque in a nervous or uncertain way but it is because one's perception of the comic is countered and balanced by perception of something incompatible with this. One may not know whether to laugh or not, but the mere fact that one is in doubt points to an awareness of comic possibilities.

It is clear that this means that any discussion of grotesque texts, if one is to show that they *are* grotesque, and why, must include the uncovering of comic patterns and structures. One must be able to see why a piece of literature is not just horrifying or disgusting or frightening, but comic as well. Whereas the reasons for the horrifying or frightening qualities of a text are usually obvious, the source of its comic effect may not be so clear. This is likely to be the case with those instances of the grotesque which are particularly brutal and hideous. Here there is the added factor of indignation and outrage in some readers' reactions to be taken into account. The German poet Gottfried Benn, in his angry young man stage, wrote some particularly nasty poems set in the dissection room of the morgue. One is entitled 'Little Aster':

> A drowned beer carter was heaved onto the table
> Someone or other had clamped a dark light lilac aster
> between his teeth.
> When, entering from the chest
> under the skin

with a long knife
I cut out the tongue and palate,
I must have bumped it, for it slid
into the brain lying alongside.
I packed it into his chest-cavity
with the sawdust stuffing
when we sewed up.
Drink your fill in your vase!
Rest in peace
little aster!

(my trans.)

This, one might say, is diabolical and satanic, but it is also a joke. The joke involves the arousing of lyrical expectations in the reader by the title, the subsequent destruction of these expectations by the sordid first line, then the justification of the title after all – a grotesque justification. Finally, it involves the application to the flower of sentiments normally reserved for dead people (whereby 'drink your fill' carries especially horrifying connotations), and a pretended sentimentality which is also grotesque in the circumstances. A response to the poem which does not include the perception of this joke aspect is, I suggest, not a full one. Worse, and this is our principal concern here, is the *refusal* to see the comic element in the poem, or the refusal, having seen it, to acknowledge its impinging, *as the comic*, on one's awareness. The latter – the suppression by the civilized and moral sensibilities of a first, immediate sense of the comic, is understandable perhaps, but should be recognized for what it is.

In drawing attention to the rather complex nature of the reader's reception of texts which carry a powerful emotional impact which may cause defence-mechanisms to cloud the initial spontaneous response, I have introduced once more the psychological question. We might ask ourselves, to pursue this line of inquiry for the moment, what are the psychological factors involved in what I have described as the classic response to the grotesque: the experience of horror (or disgust, or anger) and amusement (or glee, or delight) at the same time, the laugh which dies in the throat and becomes a grimace, or which is tinged with mild hysteria or embarrassment? The feelings of horror or disgust are psychologically straightforward, but what are the implications of laughing at a ghastly joke of the kind contained in *Little Aster*, or at one of the more drastic 'sick jokes', that contemporary popular form of the grotesque? Delight in seeing taboos flouted, a sense of momentary release from inhibitions, intellectual pleasure at seeing the joke, at perceiving the comic element, all are present. But there is also present, at least in many instances, a sadistic pleasure in the horrifying, the cruel, the disgusting. One of the most interesting writers on the grotesque, the Russian critic Mikhail Bakhtin, makes this primitive pleasure a corner-stone in his concept of the grotesque. For Bakhtin – and one finds it difficult to disagree with him – the grotesque is essentially physical, referring always to the body and bodily excesses and celebrating these in an uninhibited, outrageous but essentially joyous fashion. The carnival, that favourite popular arena for the indulging of physical excess, is seen by Bakhtin as the grotesque event *par excellence*, the place where the common people abandoned themselves to exuberantly obscene excesses of a physical kind. One can see a whole popular tradition of the grotesque here, ranging from the ancient satyr-plays to the *commedia dell'arte* (cf. Jacques Callot's marvellously grotesque illustrations of *commedia dell'arte* characters and scenes), with important links with dramatists as far apart as Aristophanes and the 'pataphysicist' Alfred Jarry, creator of the monstrously grotesque Ubu figure. It might be objected that Bakhtin's view of the grotesque is idiosyncratic and narrow (he develops it principally in connection with Rabelais, to whom it applies very well), but his insistence on the physical nature of the grotesque and on the primitive delight in what is obscene, cruel and even barbaric is quite justified. We would only wish to add that this delight constitutes only one possible aspect of the response to the grotesque.

The often intensely physical nature of the grotesque is logical when one recalls that the term was originally applied to the visual arts. Although the extension of 'grotesque' to the verbal arts occurred fairly early, the word has always been applied to the visual rather than the purely verbal. There is nothing abstract about the grotesque. I do not know of a grotesque piece of music, nor does it seem likely that the term could be legitimately applied to music, except in a very extended sense. But in that possibly most visual of all art-forms, the film, there are countless examples of the grotesque. Among the well-known contemporary film-makers (who are, collectively, as given to the grotesque as their writer colleagues), Federico Fellini perhaps stands out: his *Satyricon*, for example, is an outstandingly and consistently grotesque film.

5
Functions and Purposes
of the Grotesque

While we can make some useful generalizations about the purposes to which the grotesque may be put it is clear that the range of possible functions is very broad. Indeed, some instances of the grotesque serve no purpose at all apart from a purely ornamental or personal one. The poems by Robert Graves called 'Grotesques', of which one was quoted earlier, have no function except the fulfilment of a whimsical and capricious desire to invent something bizarre and eccentric. We might class many of the grotesque passages from *Tristram Shandy* in this category as well, although often Sterne makes satirical points through his use of the grotesque. The same may be said, as we have seen, of the work of Rabelais, whose grotesquery is sometimes satirically oriented, sometimes indulged in out of a spirit of sheer exuberance and a love of the scurrilous and extravagant.

AGGRESSIVENESS AND ALIENATION

Because of the characteristic *impact* of the grotesque, the sudden shock which it causes, the grotesque is often used as an aggressive weapon. One finds it frequently in satirical, parodistic and burlesque contexts, and in pure invective. The shock-effect of the grotesque may also be used to bewilder and disorient, to bring the reader up short, jolt him out of accustomed ways of perceiving the world and confront him with a radically different, disturbing perspective. There is probably an element of this in all instances of the grotesque, but in some cases it is most marked. Many of the uses of the grotesque in contemporary literature have this function. This effect of the grotesque can best be summed up as *alienation*. Something which is familiar and trusted is suddenly made strange and disturbing. Much of this has to do with the fundamental conflict-character of the grotesque, with the mixture of incompatibles characteristic of it. The sudden placing of familiar elements of reality in a peculiar and disturbing light often takes the form of the flinging together of disparate and irreconcilable things, which by themselves would arouse no curiosity. A rather simple illustration of this – but no less striking for that – would be Lautréamont's example of a sewing-machine and an umbrella together on an operating table.

THE PSYCHOLOGICAL EFFECT

The function of the grotesque becomes problematical when we focus our attention more narrowly on its psychological effect, and particularly when we address ourselves to the question of whether the grotesque has a liberating or an inhibiting, tension-producing effect. In the discussion of the difficult role of the comic in the grotesque it was pointed out that laughter at the grotesque is not 'free', that the horrifying or disgusting aspect cuts across our amusement: the guffaw becomes a grimace. But one can also describe this the other way round and say that our response to the horrifying is undercut by our appreciation of the comic side of the grotesque. This would suggest that the grotesque does serve to bring the horrifying and disgusting aspects of existence to the surface, there to be rendered less harmful by the introduction of a comic perspective. Kayser has put forward this view, and his notion about the grotesque 'exorcising the demonic' amounts essentially to the same thing. Similarly L. B. Jennings, in *The Ludicrous Demon* (1963), speaks of a 'disarming mechanism at work' (p. 15). In an article entitled 'Defining the Grotesque: An Attempt at Synthesis' (*Journal of Aesthetics and Art Criticism*, Summer 1970) Michael Steig tries to formulate this paradox of the grotesque: that it both liberates or disarms and creates anxiety. Steig's point of departure is the definition by Thomas Cramer (*Das Groteske bei E. T. A. Hoffmann*, 1966): 'the grotesque is the feeling of anxiety aroused by means of the comic pushed to an extreme', but conversely 'the grotesque is the defeat, by means of the comic, of anxiety in the face of the inexplicable' (p. 26, Steig's translation). Working with the Freudian notions of taboos, regression and infantile fears, Steig arrives at his own psychological definition of the grotesque:

> The grotesque involves the managing of the uncanny by the comic. More specifically: (*a*) When the infantile material is primarily threatening, comic techniques, including caricature, diminish the threat through degradation or ridicule; but at the same time, they may also enhance anxiety through their aggressive implications and through the strangeness they lend to the threatening figure. (*b*) In what is usually called the comic-grotesque, the comic in its various forms lessens the threat of identification with infantile drives by means of ridicule; at the same time, it lulls the inhibitions and makes possible on a pre-conscious level the same identification that it appears to the conscience or super-ego to prevent. In short, both extreme types of the grotesque [i.e. the predominantly threatening and the predominantly comic – P.T.] ... return us to childhood – the one attempts a liberation from fear, while the other attempts a liberation from inhibition; but in both a state of unresolved tension is the most common result, because of the intrapsychic conflicts involved.
>
> (pp. 259–60)

TENSION AND UNRESOLVABILITY

While one may not agree with some of the details of Steig's definition – in particular with the use of the word 'uncanny' – this seems a fairly plausible explanation of the psychological function of the grotesque. In particular, it accounts in psychological terms for the essential paradox of the grotesque: that it is both liberating and tension-producing at the same time. Moreover, the comic element in the grotesque is itself seen as having a dual function, exciting both 'free' and inhibited or defensive laughter. Here is a possible answer to the difficulty, discussed earlier, of pinning down the precise nature of laughter at the grotesque, and an explanation also of the frequent element of hysteria in full and spontaneous reactions to the drastically grotesque. Finally, Steig's psychological definition of the grotesque fits with and extends the structural definition offered earlier, which describes the grotesque as the unresolved clash of incompatibles in both work and effect.

We may not need such a technically psychological concept adequately to appreciate the grotesque in all cases. Often the precise nature of the conflicting elements in a work of art, and the nature of our divided response to it, are perfectly perceptible on the surface-level. But in these cases the grotesque is no less perplexing and disconcerting for that. For example we are aware of the tragic, even terrifying nature of the burial scene in *Hamlet* and (though perhaps less directly) of the porter's scene in *Macbeth*, aware at the same time of the comic aspect of these scenes, and deeply affected by the inextricable mixture which prevents us from taking them simply one way or the other and thus – since it seems part of man's nature to be satisfied only with what is certain and clear-cut – feeling content. Even more telling is the similar mixture of the tragic and terrifying with the comic in numerous scenes of *King Lear*. In the essay mentioned earlier by G. Wilson Knight, '*King Lear* and the Comedy of the Grotesque', the point is made that not only are tragic pathos and ridiculous nonsense intermingled – most clearly in the storm scenes with Lear, Edgar in his role of 'poor Tom', and the fool – but that even the barbarously cruel events of the play are not devoid of a kind of comedy that these days we would call 'black': 'Go thrust him out at gates, and

let him smell His way to Dover' is Regan's comment after Gloucester's eyes are put out. The effect of the grotesque here is to screw
even tighter the cruelty and tragedy: one's reaction to Regan's
remark would not be so intense were it not expressed in the form
of a witticism. And how are we to react, if not with a maximum of
pity and with a sense of the comic which only increases the piteous-
ness to the brink of the unbearable, to the blind Gloucester's mock-
death? Wilson Knight describes it as follows:

> They stumble on, madman and blind man, Edgar mumbling: . . . five
> fiends have been in poor Tom at once; of lust, as Obidicut; Hobbidi-
> dance, prince of dumbness; Mahu, of stealing; Modo, of murder;
> Flibbertigibbet, of mopping and mowing; who since possesses
> chambermaids and waiting-women . . .

(iv. 1. 58)

> They are near Dover. Edgar persuades his father that they are climb-
> ing steep ground, though they are on a level field, that the sea can be
> heard beneath:

Gloucester: Methinks the ground is even.
Edgar: Horrible steep.
          Hark, do you hear the sea?
Gloucester: No, truly.
Edgar: Why, then your other senses grow imperfect
          By your eyes' anguish.

(iv. 6. 3)

> Gloucester notices the changed sanity of Edgar's speech, and remarks
> thereon. Edgar hurries his father to the supposed brink, and vividly
> describes the dizzy precipice over which Gloucester thinks they stand:

                              How fearful
          And dizzy 'tis to cast one's eyes so low!
          The crows and choughs that wing the
                                        midway air
          Show scarce so gross as beetles. Halfway down
          Hangs one that gathers samphire – dreadful
                              trade; . . .

(iv. 6. 11)

Gloucester thanks him, and rewards him; bids him move off; then kneels, and speaks a prayer of noble resignation – breathing that stoicism which permeates the suffering philosophy of this play:

> O you mighty gods!
> This world I do renounce, and in your sights
> Shake patiently my great affliction off.
> If I could bear it longer and not fall
> To quarrel with your great opposeless wills,
> My snuff and loathed part of nature should
> Burn itself out.

(iv. 6. 34)

Gloucester has planned a spectacular end for himself. We are given these noble descriptive and philosophical speeches to tune our minds to a noble, tragic sacrifice. And what happens? The old man falls from his kneeling posture a few inches, flat, face foremost. Instead of the dizzy circling to crash and spill his life on the rocks below – just this. The grotesque merged into the ridiculous reaches a consummation in this bathos of tragedy.

(The Wheel of Fire, pp. 170–1)

It is the merging and intermingling of comedy and pathos which is the crucial factor in such scenes. We have to do here not with tragi-comedy in the normal sense – where a clear distinction or alternation between the comic and the tragic takes place, each keeping to its appointed realm as it were – but with the grotesque fusion of the two. Tragi-comedy points only to the fact that life is alternately tragic and comic, the world is now a vale of tears, now a circus. The grotesque, in the form it takes in a play like *King Lear*, has a harder message. It is that the vale of tears and the circus are one, that tragedy is in some ways comic and all comedy in some way tragic and pathetic. This is perhaps the most profound meaning of the grotesque, at least of that type of the grotesque exemplified by *Lear* but characteristic also of such dissimilar writers as Kafka and Beckett.

'PLAYFULNESS'

Yet it would be wrong to single out this very severe form of the grotesque as being intrinsically more valuable than others. Indeed that type of grotesqueness at the other end of the scale, so to speak, may well have claims equally valid: that is, the playful or capricious grotesque. It is likely that the play-urge, the desire to invent and experiment for its own sake, is a factor in all artistic creation, but we can expect this factor to be more than usually strong in grotesque art and literature, where the breaking down and restructuring of familiar reality plays such a large part. In addition, highly inventive and imaginative, as well as strongly experimental, literature seems to gravitate towards the grotesque. The names of Rabelais and Sterne should once again be mentioned here as representative cases, and modern experimental literature is full of the grotesque. The brothel scene from Joyce's *Ulysses* is a prime example. In connection with experimental literature the question arises as to what extent modern experimental techniques – stream of consciousness, point of view, the use of film techniques, proliferation of disparate styles and so on – themselves are related to the creation of the grotesque. Not only the work of Joyce poses this question, but also the modern American novel from Faulkner to John Barth. And, to conclude this particular list with a novel which is awe-inspiring not only for its stylistic techniques but for its radical exploration of the human mind, Elias Canetti's *Auto-da-fé* is one of the greatest examples in modern literature of what we might call the grotesque of mad invention.

Examples of the *purely* playful grotesque are difficult to find, not surprisingly since we need some sort of drastic aspect in order to feel the presence of the truly grotesque. But even authors who indulge in seemingly harmless imaginative fun can sometimes intrude into their work rather drastic elements. Those readers inclined to peruse such nursery favourites as *Alice in Wonderland* a little more closely than is normally the case may perhaps have found the occasional example of the grotesque. Indeed, 'nonsense literature' is a field where one comes across unexpected flashes of the grotesque, usually to forget them because the context is so harmless. Edward Lear's verses may seem tame, but a glance through a collection of modern limericks will serve to bring home the fact that this popular form of nonsensical (and of course off-colour) invention is a mine of the grotesque. The Germans, who have always retained in their notion of the grotesque the element of capriciousness which Vitruvius railed against in the 'original' grotesques, class their most famous nonsense poet, Christian Morgenstern, as a grotesque writer. But Morgenstern's playfulness – like Carroll and Lear, he is fascinated by language and its vagaries – has a serious side to it. He is on record as claiming that man's basically unsatisfactory relationship to his fellows, his society and the world in general stems from his being imprisoned by language, which is a most unreliable, false and dangerous thing, and that one must 'smash language', destroy man's naïve trust in this most familiar and unquestioned part of his life, before he can learn to think properly. Morgenstern's brilliantly witty games with words are thus, seen from this point of view, devious devices of alienation, and at their most radical succeed in producing in the reader a strange sensation – making one suddenly doubt one's comfortable relationship with the language – not unlike the sense of disorientation and confusion associated with the grotesque. This does not occur often, but frequently enough to give one second thoughts about the so-called purposeless, i.e. purely playful, grotesque.

THE UNINTENTIONAL GROTESQUE

The grotesque may be 'purposeless' in another sense: it may not even be intended. Examples of the unintentional or involuntary grotesque abound, in literature and art as well as in life. Even great writers are guilty of the occasional monstrous miscalculation or mis-expression, though few authors enjoy the distinction of being famous solely because of consistently and comically atrocious – and thus grotesque – work, which is the fate of the German poetess Friederike Kempner. John Cleveland went somewhat astray when, in 'Fuscara; or the Bee Errant', he described a lady's bare hand as being 'tender, as 'twere a jelly glov'd'. And such a great and dignified figure as Rainer Maria Rilke was capable, in the fifth Duino Elegy, of describing a young acrobat thus:

> Aber der junge, der Mann, als wär er der Sohn eines Nackens
> und einer Nonne; prall und strammig erfüllt
> mit Muskeln und Einfalt.

> (But the young one, the man, as if he were the son of a neck
> and a nun: tautly and robustly filled
> with muscles and simpleness.)

> (my trans.)

'The son of a neck and a nun' is such an extravagant, not to say monstrous, notion that even though we know, or deduce from the context, what Rilke means – the union of muscular strength and simple grace – we are not able to accept the figurative expression. The two things brought together are so disparate, their combination so impossible, that we withdraw from the poetic world and see the image as both obscene and ridiculous. Imagined visually – and as with all bad metaphors the literal meaning overpowers the figurative – these lines recall some grotesque detail of Bosch's 'Millennium'. Much the same is true of Cleveland's grotesque hand: the image produces the opposite of what is presumably intended because the notion of jelly covered by a glove, unattractive and bizarre enough by itself, becomes both ludicrous and nauseating when compared to the soft hand of a lady. Possibly poets are more prone to these lapses than others. Poetry is the genre which is most concerned with intense expression and metaphorical language, and many a poet, in the search for the striking phrase or novel image, has over-balanced into the ludicrous and monstrous.

The most consistent exponent of the unintentional grotesque I am aware of, however, is not a great poet. Joseph Tishler was a semi-literate contributor, under the *nom-de-plume* of Bellerive, to the Sydney *Bulletin* throughout the first half of this century. His poems were printed in the so-called 'Answers Column', which was as Douglas Stewart says in his introduction to *The Book of Bellerive* 'a kind of poetic pillory', where the most atrocious 'artistic' contributions to that journal appeared. One of Bellerive's finest gems is 'Totlinda':

> Totlinda, Totlinda,
> False queen of my heart,
> You vowed 'neath the stars
> From me you'd not part.
> When I'd cooee to thee
> From under your window,
> You'd throw me a kiss,
> Oh, faithless Totlinda!
> I paid for your shingles,
> Your wines and your dinners;
> With rapture you'd call me
> A saint among sinners.
> My God, can it be —
> That I am forsaken?
> Or is it a dream from
> Which I'll awaken?
> My heart pitter pats;
> I'm filled with emotion —
> Totlinda, adieu. I'll
> Jump into the ocean.

No doubt 'emotion' and 'ocean' have been rhymed countless times, but never, I submit, with such devastating effect.

The stage melodramas so popular in his youth seem to have been a great source of inspiration for Bellerive. We might reflect that the melodrama has certain paradoxical affinities with the farce, at least for a modern audience, and thus may provide plentiful examples of the grotesque. Certainly the melodrama as described by Bellerive bears this out:

A Woman's Revenge

Oh Wilfred why do you shun me
Appealed a woman as her blue eyes met his own
Begone Ileen said the artist
My love for thee like a bird has flown.
A cry broke from the lips of the unhappy Woman
The false deceiver had ruined her life
As he turned with contempt towards his easel
Into his side she plunged a knife.
'Twas a fatal thrust his brow turned livid
As he sank convulsively to the floor
She had fulfilled her deed of revenge and horror
Into a pool oozed the victim's gore.

Not all of the memorable examples of the involuntary grotesque come from poetry. But, leaving aside the drama where the added factor of performance introduces other difficulties, prose fiction is less likely to produce good examples of unintentional grotesquery because possible instances of it are seen in a larger context which usually diminishes, if not dissipates entirely, the impression of grotesqueness. The following passage from *Lady Chatterley's Lover*, taken in isolation, would strike many as grotesque:

He had brought columbines and campions, and new-mown hay, and oak-tufts and honeysuckle in small bud. He fastened fluffy young oak-sprays round her breasts, sticking in tufts of bluebells and campion:

and in her navel he poised a pink campion flower, and in her maiden-hair were forget-me-nots and wood-ruff.

'That's you in all your glory!' he said. 'Lady Jane, at her wedding with John Thomas.'

And he stuck flowers in the hair of his own body, and wound a bit of creeping-jenny round his penis, and stuck a single bell of a hyacinth in his navel.

(Penguin, Harmondsworth, 1960, pp. 237–8)

Some people, indeed, would aver that this is grotesque no matter what the context, pointing to the ludicrous nature of the scene (and the play made with 'forget-me-nots') but also to its tasteless nature – tasteless not because it offends against sexual taboos or decorum, but aesthetically tasteless, blatant and crass. Others, and they are perhaps the majority, would say that the quoted passage, at least in context, is touching, descriptive of a genuine and simple emotion which needs no defence. We are thus back with the eternal problem bedevilling discussions and definitions of the kind involved in literary studies: subjectivity and the inevitable variation in reader reception.

But, when talking of the unintentional or involuntary, we also become embroiled in the problem of establishing intention gene-rally. This is not a serious difficulty with the instances of the involuntary grotesque cited here, I suggest, but it is an extremely vexatious one when we come to examples, which may strike us as grotesque, from earlier ages or alien cultures. Are we justified in regarding totem-poles as grotesque when it is highly likely, indeed in many cases certain, that their creators did not feel this way about them? What was the function, and effect on whoever they were made for, of the famous stone figures on Easter Island – figures which the man accustomed to the values and criteria of Western civilization might very well class as grotesque? Even medieval gargoyles pose this problem. Those stone monsters which strike us today as both hideous and ludicrous were perhaps only hideous (or, conceivably, only ludicrous) to medieval man with his different appreciation of the world. There is considerable agreement among art critics and historians that the grotesque figures and objects which crowd Hieronymus Bosch's paintings are symbolic and not to be taken on the surface-level: does this mean that we are responding wrongly to such paintings if we see these figures and objects as grotesque? The simplest, and perhaps only practical, answer to these questions is that we are compelled, at least on one level, to view such things with the eyes of modern man and to respond to them accordingly. But we do well to remember that in the matter of aesthetic categories the classification is very much in the eye of the beholder, however much, by a process of consensus, comparison and argument, we may be able to establish certain guidelines.

Index

Select Bibliography

The number of works which deal exclusively or even largely with the grotesque is very small, although there are many which touch on the grotesque in some way. This bibliography is confined to those studies in the former category which may be of some genuine use.

BAGEHOT, WALTER, *Wordsworth, Tennyson and Browning; or Pure, Ornate and Grotesque Art in English Poetry*, in *Collected Works*, ed. N. St. John Stevas, vol. II, London, 1965.
Although somewhat narrowly Victorian, this essay is perceptive and thought-provoking, especially on the artistic temperament.

BAKHTIN, MIKHAIL, *Rabelais and His World*, trans. by Helene Iswolsky, Cambridge (Mass.), 1968.
The chapter on 'The Grotesque World of the Body' is a highly original and intelligent account of the 'exuberant' grotesque. One-sided but useful.

CLAYBOROUGH, ARTHUR, *The Grotesque in English Literature*, Oxford, 1965.
Deals only with Swift, Coleridge and Dickens. Most valuable for its history of the word 'grotesque' and summaries of other works on the subject. Clayborough's own theory should be approached with caution.

CRAMER, THOMAS, *Das Groteske bei E. T. A. Hoffman*, Munich, 1966.
A useful psychological approach to the grotesque.

FREUD, SIGMUND, *Jokes and their Relation to the Unconscious*, trans. by James Strachey, London, 1960.

The starting-point for any psychological approach to the comic, the grotesque and related matters.

HUGO, VICTOR, *Préface de 'Cromwell'* (*Theatre complet*, ed. J.-J. Thierry and J. Meleze, Paris, 1964).
This remains one of the classic statements on the grotesque and its role in literature.

GRIMM, R., JÄGGI, W., and OESCH, H. (eds.), *Sinn oder Unsinn? Das Groteske im modernen Drama*, Basel, 1962.
A general coverage of the grotesque in the modern drama; includes a useful chapter on the Italian *teatro grottesco*.

JENNINGS, LEE BYRON, *The Ludicrous Demon. Aspects of the Grotesque in German Post-Romantic Prose*, Berkeley/Los Angeles, 1963.
Has a substantial section on the nature of the grotesque (one of the best modern analyses) and a useful bibliography.

KAYSER, WOLFGANG, *The Grotesque in Art and Literature*, trans. by Ulrich Weisstein, Bloomington, 1963.
Despite its weaknesses, still a very good general introduction to the grotesque.

KNIGHT, G. WILSON, '*King Lear* and the Comedy of the Grotesque', in *The Wheel of Fire*, London, 4th ed., 1959.
Most valuable as an assessment of the role of the grotesque in a specific work of literature.

RUSKIN, JOHN, *The Stones of Venice* (vol. XI of *Works*, ed. E. T. Cook and A. Wedderburn, London, 1904).
The chapter on 'Grotesque Renaissance' is still a worthwhile account of the nature of the grotesque.

STEIG, MICHAEL, 'Defining the Grotesque: An Attempt at

Synthesis', in *Journal of Aesthetics and Art Criticism*, Summer 1970.
The most satisfactory of the psychological approaches to the grotesque.

STYAN, JOHN LOUIS, *The Dark Comedy*, Cambridge, 2nd ed., 1968.
On the 'mixture of tears and laughter' in drama from Euripides to Pinter.

SYMONDS, JOHN ADDINGTON, 'Caricature, the Fantastic, the Grotesque', in *Essays Speculative and Suggestive*, 2 vols., London/New York, 1970.
Though somewhat dated, contains some worthwhile insights.

WRIGHT, THOMAS, *A History of Caricature and Grotesque in Literature and Art*, New York, 1968.
A large survey, still valuable although it should be approached critically. This edition has a very good introduction by Frances K. Barasch, who gives one of the best modern analyses of the grotesque.

Index